Citizenship *Studies*

for OCR GCSE Short Course

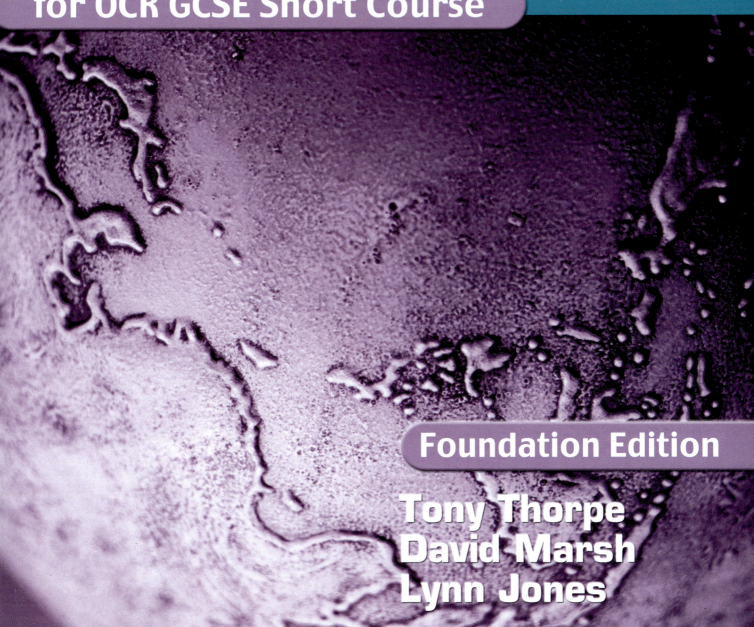

Foundation Edition

Tony Thorpe
David Marsh
Lynn Jones

With contributions from Tony Breslin, Ted Huddleston, Dan Mace, Jan Newton, Don Rowe and Carrie Supple.

INDIVIDUALS ENGAGING IN SOCIETY

Citizenship Foundation

Hodder Murray

A MEMBER OF THE HODDER HEADLINE GROUP

In this book we have, to the best of our knowledge, described the law as it stood in June 2004. However, in trying to summarise and simplify the law we have had to leave out some legal details. Therefore this book cannot be taken as proof of your legal rights. It will be important in some circumstances to seek further advice before taking any action.

The Citizenship Foundation is an independent charity which aims to empower individuals to engage in the wider community through education about law, democracy and society. Founded in 1989, the Foundation focuses particularly on developing young people's citizenship skills, knowledge and understanding.

It produces a range of publications and resources, including the award-winning Young Citizen's Passport, a practical pocket guide to the law, which can be used in conjunction with this book. Further information and details of its activities can be found on the Citizenship Foundation's website at www.citfou.org.uk

The publishers would like to thank the following individuals, institutions and companies for permission to reproduce copyright illustrations in this book:

Associated Press/Reuters: p18 (br); p74 (r) Boris Grdanoski; p77 Santiago Lyon; p20 (tl). Corbis: p74 (l) Hulton Deutsch Collection; p79 Howard Davies; p124 Wolfgang Kaehler. Rex Features: p51 Peter MacDiarmid; p60 (t) Lindsey Parnaby; p97 (r) PGI; p103 Rex. PA News: p65 Lindsey Parnaby. PA Photos: p14 Tony Harris; p18 (bl) EPA; p58 Michael Stephens; p60 (b) John Giles; p73 (r) Phil Noble; p74 EPA; p80 John Giles; p97 (l) Barry Batchelor; p97 EPA. Photofusion; p14 Gina Glover. Popperfoto: p100. Topham Picturepoint: p34 Observer. John Grooms: p67. Mary Evans Picture Library: p82. Childline: p86. Kidscape: p86. NSPCC: p86. Bristol City Council; South West News Service: p104. Mo Wilson/Format: p94. Andrew Thorpe: p32. TOGRAFOX: p88 Bob Battersby. Photodisc: p 4, 5, 6, 7, 10, 13, 15, 22, 23, 25, 28, 29, 37, 38, 39, 40, 41, 42, 43, 45, 54, 55, 61, 62, 63, 67, 68, 69, 71, 73, 75, 78, 81, 83, 85, 86, 90, 91, 92, 93, 95, 96, 99, 111, 117, 120, 121, 123, 124, 125, 126, 127, 131, 132, 133. Digital Image Ingram Publishing: p 5, 7, 9, 23, 38, 40, 43, 45, 50, 62, 69, 84, 85, 94, 95, 99, 106, 121, 123, 133. Corel: p61, 72, 75. Illustrated London News: p64, 72, 81, 118. Ikon Imaging: p12, 17, 65. Eyewire: p13, 22, 23, 65, 76, 91. ImageBoss: p7, 9, 42, 90. Think Stock: p30. Digital Vision: p 107, 123, 125. Metropolitan Police: p6. Nomad Graphique: p 7, 37, 39, 40, 54, 84, 92-3, 99, 101, 108, 113. Citizenship Foundation: p9. Letchworth Garden City Heritage Foundation: p 32, 33, 50. Council of Europe: p19.

Every effort has been made to trace and acknowledge ownership of copyright. The publishers will be glad to make suitable arrangements with any copyright holders whom it has not been possible to contact.

Note about the Internet links in the book. The user should be aware that URLs or web addresses change regularly. Every effort has been made to ensure the accuracy of the URLs provided in this book on going to press. It is inevitable, however, that some will change. It is sometimes possible to find a relocated web page, by just typing in the address of the home page for a website in the URL window of your browser.

Orders: please contact Bookpoint Ltd, 130 Milton Park, Abingdon, Oxon OX14 4SB. Telephone: (44) 01235 827720. Fax: (44) 01235 400454. Lines are open from 9.00 – 6.00, Monday to Saturday, with a 24 hour message answering service. You can also order through our website www.hoddereducation.co.uk.

British Library Cataloguing in Publication Data
A catalogue record for this title is available from the British Library

ISBN-10: 0 340 81305 9
ISBN-13: 978 0 340 81305 8

First Published 2004
Impression number   10 9 8 7 6 5 4 3 2
Year   2010 2009 2008 2007 2006 2005

Typeset by Fakenham Photosetting Ltd.
Design and artwork by Nomad Graphique.
Printed in Italy for Hodder Murray, an imprint of Hodder Education, a member of the Hodder Headline Group, 338 Euston Road, London NW1 3BH.

Contents

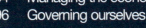

Citizenship Studies

In these introductory pages we look at the meaning of the words citizen and citizenship.

Starting out

■ What's it all about?

If you told someone at home that you had maths or French this afternoon, they would have a good idea of what you would be doing.

Maths, French and Science are subjects that have been studied at school for a long time. Everyone knows the kind of thing they cover.

Citizenship Studies is different. Some people do not know what it is. It has appeared on the curriculum only recently.

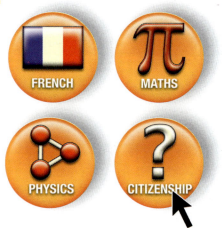

? questions

1. In small groups, write down the word citizen and then jot down any words that you think might be connected with it.

2. Share your ideas with the whole class.

3. Now use these words to write down two different statements about being a citizen. Begin each statement in the following way:
   • A citizen is . . .
   • A good citizen is . . .

■ Citizens and citizenship

Your answers probably included ideas of people taking part and belonging as well as living in society. Aristotle (a Greek writer who lived in the 4th century BC) said, 'A citizen is one who has a share in both ruling and being ruled'. This definition contains ideas of rights and responsibilities.

? question

4. Suggest an example of a right and a responsibility that someone might have.

■ Citizenship education

Citizenship education tries to give people the skills and knowledge to help them understand more about the society to which we all belong.

■ Active citizenship

A good way of learning more about how society works is to take part in some kind of practical activity. This can take place at school, or in the wider community.

If you are studying for the GCSE Citizenship Studies short course, you will be expected to write a short account of a piece of some kind of active citizenship with which you have been involved.

so...how's your citizenship?

You've probably come across quizzes like this before. How would you answer the following questions?

1 From what age will you be old enough to vote in a general election?
a) 16 years.
b) 18 years.
c) 21 years.

2 You buy a new DVD player from a local superstore. You take it home and it doesn't work. What would you do?
a) Take it back to the store.
b) Send it back to the maker.
c) Get a friend to fix it.

3 You have been working for the same company for two years. Your old boss is replaced by a new manager, who sacks you without warning. What do you do?
a) Try to get another job.
b) Confront the boss and ask why you have lost your job.
c) Take the company to an employment tribunal.

4 You discover the new trainers that you so badly want are made by overseas workers on very low wages. What do you do?
a) Refuse to buy them as a protest.
b) Buy them, but moan to the shop assistant.
c) Buy them – saying to yourself that there is not much you can do about it.

Examples of active citizenship at school might include:
- Belonging to a school council.
- Helping other students, for example, with activities such as reading schemes.
- Taking part in assemblies, plays, or mock elections.
- Helping to produce a school newsletter or magazine.
- Doing something for charity.
- Work experience.

Examples of active citizenship in the community might include:
- Writing to a newspaper, your MP or your local council about something in the community that concerns you.
- Joining a local community group.
- Doing something for charity.

■ Coursework

This is how you should write about your active citizenship:
- Title of activity.
- Your planning and organisation.
- Setting your activity into context. For example, why you are doing it, why the issue is important to you and society.
- Impact. What is the end product? What effect did you have? What impact did the activity have on you?
- Evaluation and reflection of the activity. For example, was it fun? Worthwhile? How might it have been improved? How might it be developed in the future?
- Evaluation of the process. For example, what did I learn from the experience? What were the strengths and weaknesses of the planning? Was it difficult to get people involved?

Throughout the book ideas for involvement are suggested such as:
- Joining a school council.
- Helping older or disabled people.
- Setting up schemes to prevent bullying.

 keywords

Rights
Something that a person is legally or morally entitled to. For example, people in the UK have a right not to be treated unfairly at work because of their nationality or the colour of their skin.

Responsibilities
Another word for legal or moral duties. Parents have a responsibility to make sure that their children are properly looked after.

School council
A group of pupils, normally elected by others in their class or year group. Together they make decisions or recommendations to the teaching staff about various aspects of school life.

Citizenship Studies

Answers

skills
knowledge
confidence

Your view

There is no mark scheme for the quiz on Page 5. In 1b), 18 is correct, but there are others for which two or even all three answers could be right. Picking the best answer will often depend on the circumstances at the time.

This book will give you some information, but will not tell you what you should do. It will try to encourage you to make up your own mind.

Understanding

Citizenship Studies should help you to understand more about how society works and what it means to be a member of it.

Fairness and justice

These ideas run through Citizenship Studies. They are very important when thinking about:

- how people should be treated
- how society should be organised.

Participation

Using your rights and accepting your responsibilities is not always easy. Where do you go for information or help? How do you persuade someone that you are right? How do you give useful and practical help?

Citizenship Studies will provide you with more confidence, skills and knowledge about how to become involved.

? questions

Here are some statements about what citizenship means to different people:

- 'having a vote and using it'

- 'knowing your rights and sticking up for them'

- 'looking after yourself and others'

- doing something about the things that are wrong with society'

- 'obeying the law and doing what is right'.

1. Pick one of these you most agree with and say why.

   'I think . . . is most important.'

   'My reason for this is . . .'

2. Now add a statement that sums up citizenship for you and say why you feel it does.

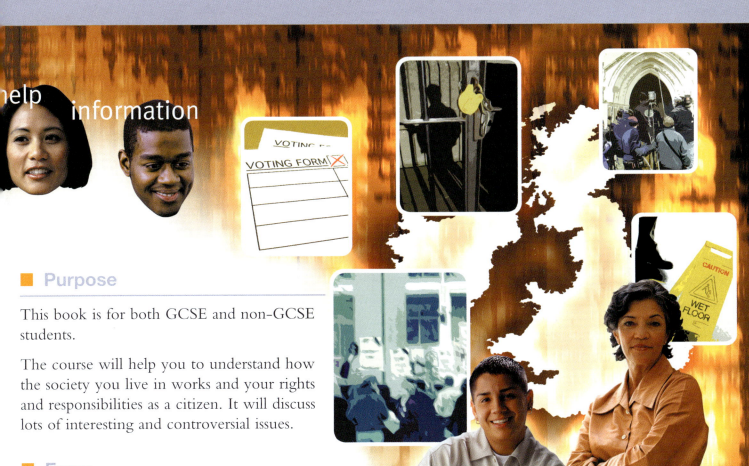

■ Purpose

This book is for both GCSE and non-GCSE students.

The course will help you to understand how the society you live in works and your rights and responsibilities as a citizen. It will discuss lots of interesting and controversial issues.

■ Exam

The book covers all you need for the OCR Citizenship Studies specification. In the final section you will be shown:

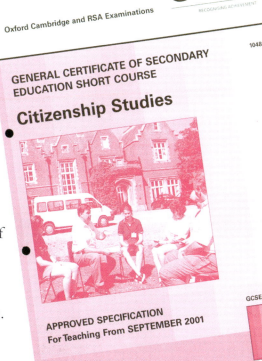

- the structure and marks for the exam
- what is expected from you in your coursework
- the differences between the three sections of the exam paper
- examples of questions and source materials.

■ More than just a subject

This book will provide you with the information you need for the exam. You could also use information from other books, the Internet, newspapers and television. In Citizenship Studies you can also use what you have learnt in other subjects such as English, history, geography, science and RE.

It's the rule

In this unit we look at the meaning of the word *law*.

Home time

Lauren got off the school bus and walked home. She rang the doorbell. Her dad opened the door and said, 'Forgotten your key again?'

Lauren stepped inside. 'Hello,' she said.

'Are you going to take your coat off?' asked her dad.

'Thank you,' said Lauren. 'Where shall I put it?'

'On the hook, of course,' her dad replied. 'Are you all right?'

'Yes, thank you,' said Lauren.

Her dad walked into the kitchen. 'Cup of tea?' he called.

'Yes, please,' answered Lauren.

'Lauren,' said her dad, looking worried, 'what's the matter? You don't usually behave like this.'

? questions

1. How would you describe Lauren's behaviour?

2. Is she behaving like:
   a) a friend?
   b) a child?
   c) a daughter?
   d) a guest?

Rules

Our behaviour with other people follows certain rules. It is easier to see the rules we follow when they are broken. Lauren was breaking unwritten rules. She was behaving like a guest, not a daughter:

Relationships

Our relationships with other people are controlled by rules. Here are some statements about marriage:

- **Age** Both partners must be aged 16 or over.
- **Faithful** A married person should not have a sexual relationship with someone else.
- **Sex** A couple should not have sex before they are married.
- **Support** A married couple should help each other.
- **Woman and man** The partners should be of the opposite sex.

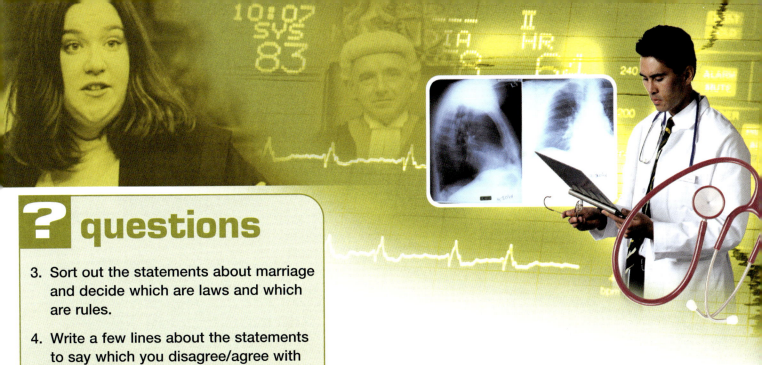

? questions

3. Sort out the statements about marriage and decide which are laws and which are rules.

4. Write a few lines about the statements to say which you disagree/agree with and why:
   - I agree with ...
   - Because ...
   - However, I disagree with ...
   - My reasoning for this is ...

Right and wrong

Many of the rules we have in society are about morality. This means what is right or wrong. Most people believe it is wrong to steal from each other. It is also against the law.

Morality versus the law

Our laws are usually the same as most people's moral beliefs, but this isn't always the case.

The case of Tony Bland In April 1989 Liverpool played Nottingham Forest in the FA Cup semi-final at Hillsborough in Sheffield. A gate was opened before the match started. Fans streamed into a very crowded part of the ground.

In the crush, 96 people were killed and many others hurt. Seventeen-year-old Tony Bland suffered serious injuries to his brain. This made him unconscious. His brain stopped working in the normal way. Although he could breathe, doctors believed he did not know what was happening around him.

Tony's family and doctors eventually decided that it would be better to allow him to die. In 1992 an application was made to court for permission to stop all his treatment.

In March 1993, the court decided it should not be against the law to remove the tube that gave him food and fluids. Nine days later, Tony died.

Some people disagreed with this because they felt that only God could end a life. They felt it was dangerous to give doctors the power to stop treatment.

? question

5. Write a description of Tony Bland's accident:
   - Tony Bland was crushed at a ...
   - He was unconscious and ...
   - His family asked for ...
   - The court decided that ...

It's the rule

What is law?

On a wider scale

Rules made by our family or school usually affect only ourselves and other people in these

Good or bad?

Many people see the law as bad. Ask your friend five words that come to mind when you say the word *law*.

groups. If we come in late, or use the wrong entrance, we aren't breaking the law – just the rule of the group or organisation.

Laws are different. They are rules that apply in all situations, to everyone within the community, although some laws don't affect children.

? questions

1. Explain the difference between rules and laws. Give an example of each.

2. Draw a picture of what the law means to you. Share your ideas with the whole class.

3. Why might people have a bad view of the law?

Civil and criminal law

Law can be divided into *civil* and *criminal* law.

Civil law gives people ways of settling disagreements and dealing with certain events. For example:

- divorce
- unfair treatment at work
- buying or selling a house
- sorting out arguments between neighbours.

If you buy something that doesn't work or doesn't do what the shop assistant claimed, it is civil law you use to get your money back.

Criminal law covers behaviour that the state thinks is wrong. The police are usually involved. For example:

- violence, such as assault or murder
- theft and burglary
- sexual offences, such as rape
- traffic offences, such as speeding or driving without insurance.

Dear Chloe

I thought that I'd write a note in the Christmas card to let you know our news over the last year – it is not good!

In January, Dean passed his driving test and bought a car. Since then he has a conviction for speeding and two parking fines.

In April, Madeline was caught shoplifting. She was meant to be in school. She was arrested and taken to the police station.

In July, my brother seriously hurt his hand at work. He works on a farm and the farmer had not replaced the guard on the cutting blade. His union is trying to get him compensation.

In August, my divorce from John was finalised.

In September, I had problems with my neighbour. She refused to cut down trees that blocked the light.

In October, I lost my job. They said I was not up to standard. I have worked there for ten years. I am making a claim for unfair dismissal.

Since then things have been better. However, last week my car was broken into and my mobile phone stolen.

Much love,

Anna XX

? questions

4. Read Anna's letter and decide whether the things she describes refer to civil or criminal law. The first two are done for you.

Criminal	Civil
• Speeding fine • Parking fine	

5. Explain what civil and criminal law are in your own words.

The law machine

This unit explains where our laws come from and how they are made and changed.

Law makers

■ Development

The law in England and Wales has been developed in three ways:

- by Parliament
- by judges in court
- through our links with Europe.

Laws in Northern Ireland and Scotland are sometimes different.

■ Parliament

The government that is elected makes laws based on its policies. These are called statutes or Acts of Parliament.

For example, before the 2001 general election, the Labour Party promised to get tough on offenders. After the election, they introduced the *Proceeds of Crime Bill*, which allowed courts to take money gained through crimes such as drug dealing.

New laws can also be put forward by individual Members of Parliament. These are called private members' Bills. Only a few ever become law: for example, the *Abortion Act 1967,* which is an instance of a private members' Bill that became law.

Judge-made law

Over the years decisions made by judges have been written down. This is called 'common law'.

Today, when a judge hears a case in court, lawyers tell him or her of similar cases. The judge will follow the decision of a senior or equal-ranking judge in an earlier case. If a senior judge believes a ruling is out of date, he or she may change the law. For example, in 1991 a man was charged with rape after having sex with his wife against her will. His lawyers said he wasn't guilty because the law said it was not rape if a man forced his wife to have sex. Five senior judges disagreed. They said this was out of date and that the law should change. A man can now be found guilty of raping his wife.

Freedom of Information Act 2000

CHAPTER 36

Explanatory Notes have been produced to assist in the understanding of this Act and are available separately

■ Europe

Never again After the Second World War (1939–45) many people felt that the countries in Europe should work together much more closely, so that such a terrible war should never happen again. Two organisations were set up to do this. These are the **European Union** and the **Council of Europe**.

European Union The origins of the European Union go back to 1951 with a treaty between Belgium, France, Germany, Italy, Luxembourg and the Netherlands. A number of states joined in 2004, and today the European Union has 25 nations, including the UK.

Each state agreed that European law would become part of its national law.

European law is mainly to do with employment, transport, agriculture, environment and trade.

The Council of Europe This organisation is concerned with human rights and international understanding. One of its most important achievements has been setting up the European Convention on Human Rights. Britain signed this in 1951. In 2000 these rights became part of UK law when the *Human Rights Act* became law. The Convention is looked at in more detail on page 19.

 question

1. Complete the following: The European Union is a group of _____. These nations want to work more closely together after Europe was torn apart in _____.

❖ keywords

Bill
The suggested wording for a law which is discussed and approved by Parliament.

Parliament
The House of Commons and the House of Lords.

The law machine

Parliamentary process

Government policy

When the Government wants to change the law it introduces a new Bill in Parliament. In the 1980s the Conservative Government felt that the actions of trade unions were holding British industry back. They passed a number of laws reducing trade union power.

Involving people

The Government talks to people who know about the area covered by the new law. A Green Paper sets out the main ideas for change. This is followed by a White Paper, which has more definite ideas. Members of the public can give their views to their Member of Parliament (MP) or the government department involved.

Pressure

Sometimes new laws are passed because of public pressure.

In November 2000, the age of consent for male gay sex was lowered to 16, bringing it into line with the heterosexual age of consent. This happened after a long campaign by many groups of people to change the law.

Trade union march – early 1980s.

Demonstration for gay rights, June 1998.

Stages of a Bill

A Bill normally starts in the **House of Commons**, where it is debated by MPs.

First Reading
The Bill is introduced to Parliament. The title is read out and a date fixed for the Second Reading.

Second Reading
The main ideas behind the Bill are debated in Parliament.

The law was recently changed to provide people over 75 with free TV licences. In the Second Reading there was a debate on the strengths and weaknesses of this idea.

Once a Bill has passed its Second Reading, there is a good chance that it will become law.

Committee Stage
A small group of MPs or members of the House of Lords go through the Bill checking everything in fine detail.

Report Stage and Third Reading
The Bill then moves back to the whole House, where the Committee reports on the changes it has made.

The Report Stage is followed by the Third Reading, when the House of Commons votes on this final version of the Bill.

The Bill is then passed to the House of Lords, where it is examined in much the same way. Any changes it suggests are sent back to the House of Commons for it to look at.

The Lords can delay a Bill for up to a year, but cannot prevent it from becoming law.

Royal Assent
The Bill goes to the Queen or King to be 'signed'. This is traditional, but the Queen or King does not actually sign or comment on it her- or himself. The Bill is then an Act.

keywords

European Court of Human Rights
The court that decides on cases where it is claimed human rights have been broken. It is based in Strasbourg in France.

House of Commons
The part of Parliament made up of elected MPs.

House of Lords
The section of Parliament mainly made up of people specially appointed, and not elected. They are given the title of 'Lord'. Some are judges or bishops.

The law machine

Judge-made law

WE HAVEN'T COME ACROSS *THIS* BEFORE!

◼ Getting on line

Almost every major company in Britain has a website. Usually its web address is based on its name: e.g. Cadbury or Kellogg's.

Anyone who wants their own website address can pay to register their chosen name.

Some people have registered names that are not their own, which they believe they can sell to others.

In the 1990s, Marks & Spencer, Sainsbury's and Virgin learnt that a group of dealers in Internet names had registered their companies' names without their agreement. They were hoping to sell the names back to the company or to someone else. A chain of burger restaurants had been asked for £25,000 to buy back its name.

? question

1. Write an email to a friend giving your view on this practice.
   'I feel it is right/wrong to set up website addresses that are not your own because _____'

Off line? The companies felt it was wrong that they should have to buy back a name they had used for years. They believed their business and reputation could be badly damaged if the name was sold to someone else. They decided to take their case to court to get their money back.

Problem Judges base decisions on earlier cases. This is called precedent. The problem the judges faced was that the Internet was new. The courts had never had a case like this before. There was no precedent on how this should be judged.

Solution The dealers were ordered to give back the names to the companies on which they were based.

Judge-made law The judges had made a new piece of law. This will stand until overruled by a higher court, or a new law is passed by Parliament.

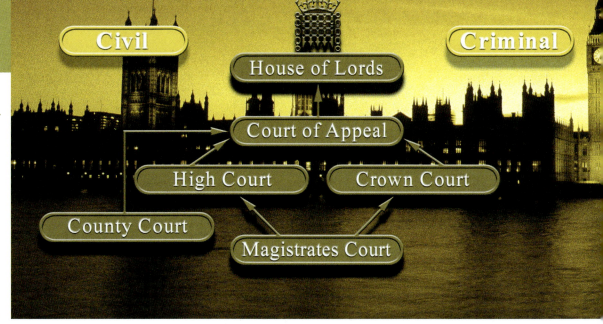

Civil

Criminal

House of Lords

Court of Appeal

High Court

Crown Court

County Court

Magistrates Court

■ Precedent

The word 'precede' means to go before. 'Precedent' is the name given to the system where judges follow decisions made in previous cases where the facts are the same. If a decision of a court is challenged, the case will be taken to a higher court, normally the Court of Appeal. Here the judges will apply decisions already made by the Court of Appeal or the House of Lords, which is at the top of the court structure.

The House of Lords may follow its own past decisions or create new law. This is called case law.

■ Unelected lawmakers

In the United States, many judges are elected by local communities. In England and Wales they are lawyers appointed by the Queen or King on the advice of the Lord Chancellor – a senior lawyer and a member of the Government.

- In England and Wales almost all senior judges are men.
- Two out of 33 judges who work in the Court of Appeal are women.
- There are few women judges in the House of Lords.
- There are few black or Asian judges working in the High Court, the Court of Appeal or the House of Lords.
- Most judges were educated in fee-paying schools.
- Very few are below 50 years of age.

? questions

2. Do you think it matters that there aren't any women, black or Asian judges in the House of Lords? Give reasons for your answer.

3. You have a brief meeting with your MP. Tell him or her how you would try to make judges more like other people in the community.
   - 'I think that judges should . . .'

The law machine

Human rights law

On 1 September 1939, Warsaw in Poland was bombed by Germany. This lasted for 27 days before the city fell.

On 25 September, German planes bombed the city again, setting whole streets on fire and 12,000 people were killed.

On 22 July 1942, Germany began to get rid of the Jews. By 12 September, 310,322 men, women and children had been sent to death camps and gassed.

On 19 April 1943, the German army set fire to the part of Warsaw where the Jews lived. On 16 May, Hitler was told that this district no longer existed.

▮ The United Nations

United Nations peacekeepers in Sierra Leone, West Africa.

During the Second World War, 50 million people died and almost every country suffered the effects of war.

After the war, 51 countries came together to form the United Nations to try to make sure that nothing like this ever happened again. Today the UN is an international organisation. Most countries of the world belong to it. It works to stop wars and keep peace and security.

The Universal Declaration of Human Rights

In 1948, the United Nations drew up the Universal Declaration of Human Rights. This sets out basic human rights that apply to everyone.

Rights listed in the Declaration include:

- protection from arrest without good reason
- the right to a fair trial
- freedom of thought, conscience and religion
- freedom to meet together in a group
- the right to education.

The Declaration is important but does not have the force of law.

UN Human Rights Commission

The United Nations Human Rights Commission investigates cases where governments are suspected of abusing people's human rights. People accused of

Slobodan Milosevic, former Yugoslav President, was put on trial in the Hague.

abusing human rights are put on trial at an International Criminal Tribunal in the Hague.

European Convention on Human Rights

The European Convention on Human Rights was written after the end of the Second World War, and it is meant to protect human rights. Most of the rights it includes are set out on pages 22–3.

Unlike the UN Declaration, the European Convention gives governments and individuals a way to seek justice if they feel their rights have been broken. They can take their case to the European Court of Human Rights in Strasbourg, France. If the Court agrees, it can give damages to the person who brought the case. The country involved will then have to change its law so that it no longer breaks the Convention. This has happened several times in Britain.

Corporal Punishment in Schools In September 1976, Jeffrey Cosans took a short cut through a cemetery on his way home from school. This was against the rules. It was reported to the head teacher. He wanted to punish Jeffrey with the strap. Jeffrey refused and was supported by his parents. Jeffrey was excluded from school.

Eventually, the head said that Jeffrey could come back, but could not promise that Jeffrey would not be hit if he misbehaved again. Jeffrey did not return to school.

Jeffrey's mother believed the school had broken the European Convention on Human Rights. His parents took the case to the European Court of Human Rights. The Court agreed. It found that the United Kingdom had broken the Convention by not respecting the parents' objections to corporal punishment.

After this judgement, the British government had to change the law. In 1987, corporal punishment was banned in state schools and in all private schools in 1999.

? questions

1. The United Nations has the job of trying to keep world peace. What difficulties do you think it faces in doing this?

2. Give one argument for and one against having international agreements such as the European Convention of Human Rights.

Human Rights Act 1998

The only time this is not necessary is during war or in other national emergencies.

Public bodies All public bodies such as local authorities, hospitals, schools and the police must carry out their work in line with the Convention.

The long route

The United Kingdom was the first country to sign the European Convention on Human Rights. However, every British government since 1953 has not been willing to make this part of our law because it threatens Parliament's right to decide the law.

Anyone who wanted to force a right under the Convention had to take the case to the European Court of Human Rights. This was long and difficult. One case took nine years to progress through the system.

All change

After winning the 1997 general election, the Labour Party decided to make the Convention part of UK law. In 1998 the *Human Rights Act* was passed. It became law in 2000. Almost all rights in the European Convention are now part of UK law. These rights are listed on pages 22–23. But what does this really mean?

All laws Under the *Human Rights Act* all UK laws must be in line with the Convention.

Human Rights Act 1998

CHAPTER 42

ARRANGEMENT OF SECTIONS

Introduction

The Convention Rights.
Interpretation of Convention rights.

Legislation

Interpretation of legislation.
Declaration of incompatibility.
Right of Crown to intervene.

Public authorities

Acts of public authorities.

Terrorism Countries do not have to follow the Convention times of emergency. The Unite Kingdom can either hold or deport people whom it regards a terrorist threat.

Getting the right balance

The parts of the European Convention on Human Rights that are in the *Human Rights Act* are on pages 22–23.

Some of the rights cannot be changed by the State. These are in Articles 2, 3, 4, 7 and 14. For example, torture (Article 3) is never acceptable.

However, the rights in Articles 8, 9, 10 and 11 may be restricted for reasons of public safety or to protect the rights of others.

In these situations a court must decide. Usually this involves balancing the rights.

For example, in 2001 the High Court had to decide whether newspapers could report where the two boys who murdered the toddler Jamie Bulger lived after they had been released from prison.

It was argued that newspapers had the right to print the information, but that the boys could face the risk of serious injury if people knew their addresses.

Here the right to freedom of expression (Article 10) is competing with the right to life (Article 2). The judge had to decide whether the right to freedom of expression was more important than the right of the boys to live in safety.

A right to privacy In 2001 the *Daily Mirror* published a photograph of the model Naomi Campbell going to a meeting of Narcotics Anonymous – a support group to help drug addicts.

Naomi Campbell said that the paper had no right to print information about such a personal problem.

The newspaper said that, because her career depended on publicity, she lost her right to privacy. It also said that Ms Campbell had said she did not take drugs. This was not true.

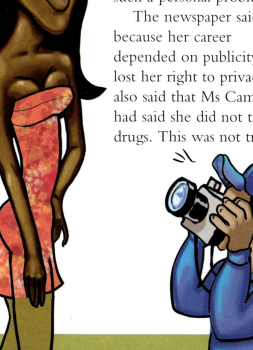

? questions

1. In what situations do you think it would be reasonable to limit a person's right to (a) free speech and (b) meet or gather with who they wish? Explain why.

2. Which right do you think was stronger? Naomi Campbell's right to privacy or the newspaper's right to tell people about her drug treatment?

The European Convention on Human Rights

These parts of the European Convention on Human Rights are included in the *Human Rights Act 1998.*

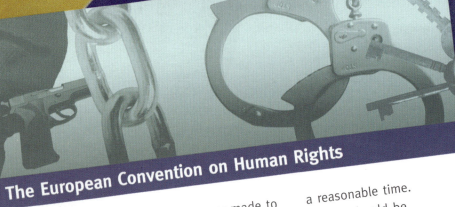

The European Convention on Human Rights

Article 2
Right to life
Everyone has the right to have their life protected by law. Taking a life is acceptable only when it is absolutely necessary, such as in self-defence or to protect the life of someone else.

Article 3
Prohibition of torture
Everyone has the right to be free from torture.

Article 4
Prohibition of slavery and forced labour
No one shall be held in slavery or made to do forced labour. This right does not apply to work related to the military, prison or community service.

Article 5
Right to liberty and security
Everyone has the right not to have their freedom taken away, unless it is within the law and the proper legal practices are followed.

Article 6
Right to a fair trial
Everyone has the right to a fair trial and public hearing within a reasonable time. People should be treated as innocent until proved guilty.

Article 7
No punishment without law
No one should be found guilty of an offence that was not a crime when it took place. Nor should they receive a heavier punishment than was normally given when the offence was committed.

The European Convention on Human Rights

Article 8
Right to respect for a person's private and family life
Everyone has the right to respect for their private and family life, their home and their mail.

Article 10
Freedom of expression
Everyone has the right to express an opinion. This may be limited for reasons of public safety or to protect the rights of others.

Article 12
Right to marry
Men and women have the right to marry, but there are laws about whom you may or may not marry and where a marriage may take place.

Article 9
Freedom of thought, conscience and religion
Everyone is free to hold whatever views and beliefs they wish. Their right to say what they think may be restricted in certain circumstances.

Article 11
Freedom of assembly and association
Everyone has the right to get together with other people in a peaceful way. This includes the right to form and join a trade union.

Article 14
Prohibition of discrimination
Everyone is entitled to the rights and freedoms set out in the Convention, whatever their race, sex, language, religion, politics, national or social origin, birth or other status.

The rights in Articles 8–11 can be restricted to protect things such as public safety or the rights of others, or to stop crime. Someone who feels that a right has been taken away unfairly can complain to a Court. The Court will decide whether the complaint is reasonable.

A number of further points were added to the Convention. These are called protocols.

Convention on Human Rights

Article 2
Right to education
No one shall be deprived of the right to education. The state must respect the right of parents to an education for their child that fits their religious and general beliefs.

Article 3
Right to free elections
Elections for government must be free and fair and must take place by secret ballot.

Protocol 1 Article 1
Protection of property
No one shall have their possessions taken away except in limited circumstances. These allow, for example, the State to take money for the payment of taxes or to take goods that are unlawful or dangerous.

Protocol 6 Articles 1 & 2
Getting rid of the death penalty
No one shall be condemned to death or executed. However, the state may bring in the death penalty at times of war or threat of war.

Consumer rights

This unit outlines the law covering many of the things that we buy every day.

Contract

Almost every time we buy **goods** or **services** we enter into a contract.

This is a legal agreement where someone agrees to provide goods or services for someone else – usually, for money.

Every time we buy something from a shop, a contract is made between the shop owner and ourselves.

A contract can also be made even if nothing is said. Buying goods on the Internet is an example of this.

A

B

C

Failing to deliver

If what you have bought doesn't work properly or is not what you were promised, it means that the shop has failed to keep its side of the contract.

In this situation the law says that you are entitled to your money back or **compensation**.

? question

1. Look at the pictures above and decide, in each case, whether a contract has been broken and, if so, by whom.

What if . . . ?

A
- the customer complains that the coffee is cold?
- the customer decides she would rather have tea?

B
- the customer buys the PC, but later decides that she can't afford it?
- the customer has to wait much longer for the computer to be delivered than she expected?

C
- the customer wishes to change the carton of orange juice for a cheaper brand?
- the checkout assistant realises that the drinking chocolate has been wrongly priced, and tells the customer she will have to pay £2 more?

◼ Disappointment

Elaine and Gary booked their honeymoon in the Dominican Republic. The brochure said everything was included in the price.

'Every single gin and tonic and snack has been paid in advance,' claimed the brochure.

'All leisure activities, like archery, scuba diving and the gym, are completely free.'

When they got to the hotel, the service that they received was not what they had expected.

'Just after we arrived,' Elaine explained, 'we were given a list of everything that was free. The trouble was, it didn't match the brochure.'

Things not as expected:

- The first scuba diving lesson was free. After that it cost £30 an hour.
- Only four free alcoholic drinks were allowed. They had to be paid for after 11 pm.
- There was no archery.
- The gym had only a couple of cycling machines and a sun lounger.

The cost of the fortnight's holiday was £2,500. Elaine and Gary paid another £400 to do everything they had planned.

When they complained to the manager, he said that the holiday that they had booked had been withdrawn in December – but that the tour operator was continuing to offer it.

 question

2. Write a letter from Elaine and Gary to the tour operator complaining about the holiday.

Paragraph 1
Details of the holiday. Place, cost, what they thought was included.

Paragraph 2
What they didn't get that they thought they were getting.

Paragraph 3
What they did about it at the time.

Paragraph 4
What they expect the tour operator to do about it, and what they will do next if they don't get what they want.

❖ keywords

Compensation
A sum of money to make up for loss or damage a person suffers.

Goods
Items or possessions.

Services
Work that is done for payment, such as hairdressing, plumbing or repairs to a car.

Consumer rights

When things go wrong

■ As we were

For hundreds of years there have been laws to protect the quality and price of things that people buy. The sale of things people need, such as bread, meat and fuel, has almost always been controlled by law.

However, anyone buying something else – such as a horse or a cart – had very little protection in law. If the horse was sick or the cart fell to pieces, there was little a buyer could do. This is where the phrase '*caveat emptor*', meaning 'buyer beware', comes from. It is still used today. It is important when buying something privately, such as a car.

Best before In 1350, a Londoner, Richard Quelhogge, bought, for four pence, a pig that he found lying by the side of the Thames. Richard cut off the legs of the animal and tried to sell them.

Richard was found guilty in court for selling stinking meat.

■ Changing times

In the nineteenth century more goods were made in factories. But when these didn't work it was very difficult for people to get their money back.

One problem was the law. There were no rules, setting out people's rights and responsibilities. To deal with this Parliament passed a whole series of Acts in the late 1800s.

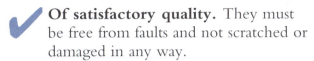

■ Today

During the twentieth century the law continued to change.

The law we use today is the *Sale of Goods Act 1979*. This states that all goods sold by a trader must be:

✔ **Of satisfactory quality.** They must be free from faults and not scratched or damaged in any way.

✔ **Fit for their purpose.** The goods must do what they are designed to do and, what the sales assistant or the packaging claims.

✔ **As described.** They must be the same as they are described in an advertisement, on the packaging or by the sales assistant.

Problems Complaints about faulty goods should be made to the place from which they were bought. The contract is with the shop, not the manufacturer.

If the goods are not satisfactory, customers have the right to have their money back in full.

Time There is no set time limit in which goods must be returned, but it is important to tell the seller about the problem as soon as possible.

If someone buys a personal stereo that doesn't work properly, but uses it, knowing it is faulty, they are seen to have accepted the goods. This makes it much harder to claim a refund.

? question

1. Apply the *Sale of Goods Act 1979* to each of the following situations:

Peter buys a CD over the Internet. When it arrives he discovers that it is the wrong one.

Chris buys a new battery for his watch. It is the wrong size.

Lena buys a new television. The television works but the casing is scratched.

Jasmine buys a wardrobe for her daughter. On the packaging it says it is easy to put together, but the instructions are difficult to follow. Jasmine is unable to complete the job.

IS IT TOO LATE TO *RETURN* THIS?

Consumer wrongs

This unit explains some of the criminal aspects of consumer law.

Mott the who?

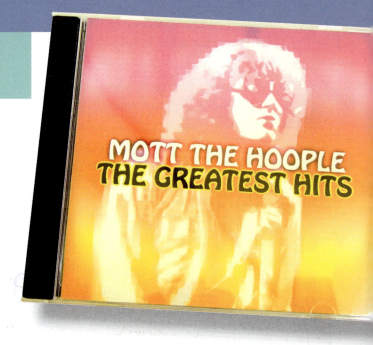

Phil is a fan of the 1970s pop group Mott the Hoople. He bought their greatest hits CD.

When he listened to it, he realised that it was not the real Mott the Hoople.

Phil told the group's management. They got in touch with the local **trading standards department.**

The record company had bought the recordings from someone who said they were made by the original band. The CD bought by Phil was not as described, so – under the *Sale of Goods Act 1979* – he got his money back from the shop.

■ A criminal offence

In falsely describing the CD, the record company had committed a criminal offence. They were charged, under the *Trade Descriptions Act 1968*, with supplying a CD with a false description. They were fined £8,000.

? question

1. Tell Phil's story in your own words. Include these words in your story:
   - Mott the Hoople CD
   - trading standards department
   - Sale of Goods Act
   - Trade Descriptions Act.

Dangerous goods

It is a criminal offence to sell something that is:

- dangerous
- below the safety standards required by law.

■ A tragic accident

Chloe, aged three, was playing on a children's slide in the garden at home. Her head became trapped between the top of the slide and a metal support. Her mother rushed her to hospital. But Chloe died six days later.

The company that made and sold the slide was charged with selling an unsafe toy.

Evidence Here are some of the facts and statements that were given at the trial:

A The company had made and sold 200,000 slides before this accident happened.

B As soon as it heard about Chloe's accident, the company took the slide from sale. Sixteen days later it was on sale again but with changes to make it safer.

C/ Safety experts said the slide met British safety standards.

D) A director of the company said, 'This slide has an excellent safety record. We have never had a serious accident or a death with any item before.'

(E) Chloe's mother said, 'I had been with Chloe in the garden watching her play on the slide. I then went into the house. After a while I realised that I couldn't hear her. I looked out of the window and saw Chloe hanging from the slide'.

F The company now offer a safety kit for people who bought the slide before the accident.

G A safety expert said, 'It is not always possible to know what young children will do.'

? questions

2. In court, the judge had to decide whether the company was guilty of selling an unsafe toy. Some of the evidence heard in the court is listed on the left.

   Which pieces of evidence (A–G) would help the judge to decide whether or not the company had sold an unsafe toy?

3. You are the judge in this case. Explain what your judgement would be and why.
   - In this case I think that . . .
   - My evidence for this is . . .
   - However, I would like to make the point that . . .

❖ keywords

Trading standards department
People employed by the local authority to check that local shops and businesses are not breaking the law in the way that they trade. If the department believes that an offence has been committed, they can prosecute the trader.

Consumer complaints

In this unit we look at ways of making a complaint.

Taking action

Washed up

Therese O'Dell bought an expensive new washing machine. It broke down after six months. She rang the shop where she bought it. They told her to call the manufacturer's help line, who said an engineer would come.

It took three weeks for someone to come. Then they left – saying that new parts were needed.

A week later the parts were put in. But the washing machine soon broke down again.

It took another week before anyone came. The engineer told Mrs O'Dell that the same parts needed replacing. They would take a further week to be delivered.

? questions

1. Put the heading 'Mrs O'Dell's washing machine' and make a list of all the problems she had with the machine.

2. Suggest three things she could do to get the washing machine sorted out. Which would be the best and why?

Problems

The difficulties that people face when things go wrong are rarely straightforward.

Adam I bought a new computer, with a printer, for £1,300. The sales assistant said it would be able to print up to eight pages a minute. It sometimes takes five minutes to do a single page.

I rang the printer manufacturer. They said that I'd been sold the wrong printer for my computer. The right one will cost me £140.

The shop I bought it from refuse to help. They won't take the old printer because it has been used and cannot be resold.

Sairah I took four films of my holiday in for developing. When I went to collect them, two of the films had been lost. They offered me just under £10 – the cost of replacing the film.

I said that this was not enough – but they pointed to the small print on my receipt. This said the company will only pay the replacement cost of the film.

Alex I bought a video recorder from a shop in town. It was reduced because the model was not made any more. I found that the instruction booklet had been used and someone else's TV licence was inside the box!

Louisa My son was eating a piece of bread pudding when he found a screw in his mouth. I'd bought it for £1.79 from the local supermarket.

Clive I bought my car through an advert in the local paper. The man said it was a good runner. I paid him £4,200. It was fine for the first couple of weeks. Now it needs a new clutch and gearbox, which will cost about £1,000. I've written to ask him for £500 – which I thought was fair – but he's ignored my letter.

Yvonne I ordered a new bath. The shop said it would cost £340. This week they called to say that the factory had put its prices up. If I want the bath I will have to pay another £120.

? question

3. Give advice to each person. Set it out like this:

Sairah's case
- a brief description of the case
- the position in law
- the action you think she should take.

Consumer complaints

Problem solving – a guide

■ First things

Take it back Many shops will exchange faulty goods straightaway.

Ask to see the manager Sometimes it helps to ask to see someone in a senior position.

Write a letter Write to the company head office explaining why you are unhappy.

Keep a record Keep a record of all you have done, with dates. Keep copies of all letters.

■ Finding help

Citizens Advice Bureau These are advice centres, usually known as CABs, which give free help and advice. They have offices in most towns and cities. Their number is in the local phone book.

citizens advice bureau

Small-claims courts Anyone over 18 unable to get satisfaction over a problem can try to get their money back by putting their case to a judge in a county court.

There is no need for a lawyer. It is a simple and cheap way of settling a case up to the value of £5,000.

Solicitors These are lawyers able to give advice on legal issues.

Trading standards departments Sometimes known as consumer protection departments, these give advice to the public about all kinds of consumer problems. However, their main job is to check that shops and traders keep within the law.

■ The law

Sale of Goods Act 1979
This states that all goods sold by a trader must be (see page 27):

McFadden & Taylor

- of satisfactory quality
- fit for their purpose
- as described.

Supply of Goods and Services Act 1982

This states that a service must be provided:

- with reasonable care and skill
- within a reasonable time
- at a reasonable cost, if no price has been agreed in advance.

Consumer Credit Act 1984

If there's a fault with something bought using a credit card,

OF SATISFACTORY QUALITY!

FIT FOR THEIR PURPOSE!

AS DESCRIBED!

the customer may be able to claim from the credit card company (applies only to goods costing more than £100).

Unfair Contract Terms Act 1977

The wording or small print of a customer's contract must be fair. If it is not, the customer can ask a court to overturn it.

For example, a security firm said it would not be responsible if the alarm failed and the house was burgled. This, a court decided, was unfair. The customer was paid compensation.

Trade Descriptions Act 1968

It is a criminal offence for traders to make false claims about what they are selling.

Consumer Safety Act 1987

It is a criminal offence for a trader to sell goods that are not safe. The law applies to both new and second-hand goods.

Anyone suffering injury or damage from unsafe or dangerous goods can claim damages from the manufacturer.

? question

1. Match the following descriptions to the six Acts described above:

a. It is a criminal offence for a trader to make false claims

b. The wording of contracts must be fair

c. It is a criminal offence to sell goods which are not safe

d. Goods must be of satisfactory quality, fit for purpose and as described

e. A service must be provided with care and skill

f. If there is a fault with something bought by a credit card, the customer may be able to claim from the credit card company.

IT DOES WHAT IT SAYS ON THE TIN!

Looking for work

This unit looks at the rights and responsibilities of employers and employees at work.

On the move

Almost everyone living in Britain today has origins elsewhere.

Romans, Saxons, Vikings and Normans came to Britain to invade and conquer. Others, such as people from Africa, were brought by force as slaves and servants. Refugees from France, Germany, Russia and other parts of Europe came to Britain to escape persecution and violence in their own countries.

■ A better life

The other reason many people came to Britain has been the hope that they, or their children, would find a better standard of living. This is called economic migration and goes back as early as 1130 AD.

■ Skills

Many **migrants** bring useful skills.

- Merchants from France brought an understanding of money and trade. They started London's banking and financial services.
- Weaving, printing, brewing and engineering were brought by the French, Germans and Dutch.

■ Filling a gap

After the Second World War, there was the huge task of rebuilding Britain, damaged by six years of war.

London Transport set up centres in the West Indies to recruit bus crews. Textile and engineering firms in the north of England and Midlands sent agents to find workers in India and Pakistan.

For about 25 years, people from the West Indies, India, Pakistan and, later, Bangladesh travelled to work and settled in Britain.

Arriving from Jamaica, June 19

Clinton Edwards I joined the RAF and came over to England in 1942. When I went back to Jamaica there was no work. So I decided to return to England, where there were more jobs.

Sher Azan I came to Britain from Pakistan in 1961, when I was 20. There were better job opportunities over here. In fact, British companies placed advertisements for work in our local newspaper.

■ Two-way traffic

Britain has also been a country that many people have left. People have left to settle in parts of Africa, the United States, Canada, Australia and New Zealand.

■ The importance of the Commonwealth

The British Empire once included much of Africa, India and Australasia. Since 1945, almost all these countries have become independent and together form a group called the Commonwealth, with the Queen as its head.

Over the last fifty years many people from Commonwealth countries have come to settle in Britain, and people in Britain have moved to Commonwealth countries. This has been helped by having English as a common language, and some similarities in our way of life.

EMIGRATION TO NEW ZEALAND PARADISE

Every industrious young man or woman in good health will, on approval, receive a FREE GIFT of Forty Acres of Good Land in the province of Auckland, New Zealand, together with Forty Acres more for each person above 18 years AND Twenty Acres for each child above five.

? questions

1. Write a short explanation of why we are now a country which includes many different races. Include the following points:
    *   Most people here today have origins elsewhere.
    *   People come here for a better life and to escape persecution.
    *   People bring useful skills.
    *   We have a shortage of labour.
    *   We have links with the Commonwealth.

2. If you had an opportunity to move to another country to work:
    *   Where would you choose and why?
    *   What problems would you have?
    *   Who would be responsible for your safety and wellbeing?

3. Explain what the Commonwealth is in your own words.

✦ keyword

Migrant
Someone moving from one place or country to another. An emigrant is a person who leaves their region or country. Immigrant refers to a person arriving *from* another region or country.

Looking for work

Race discrimination

■ Prejudice

Suzanne Jones, a black English woman, applied to work in a solicitors' office. She was well qualified. After an interview with Mr Wheeler, she was not offered the job.

Six weeks later, Suzanne saw an advertisement for a similar job at the same firm. She phoned to say she was interested.

She went for another interview. Mr Wheeler recognised her. He became very upset. He asked her to leave.

Suzanne believed that she was being rejected because she was black. She called Mr Wheeler a bigot – and left.

Mr Wheeler then interviewed Deborah Cook, who was white. During the interview he said to Deborah, 'A coloured girl applied for the job. Why would I want to take her on, when English girls are available?'

Deborah was offered the job, but turned it down. She told someone in the local race relations office what Mr Wheeler had said.

■ Advice

Suzanne knew that racial discrimination was against the law. She went to see a solicitor, who said that she believed Mr Wheeler had broken the *Race Relations Act*. Suzanne could take her case to an **employment tribunal**. If they decided that Mr Wheeler had broken the law, Suzanne might get compensation for being unfairly turned down.

■ Tribunal

Mr Wheeler told the tribunal that he had not discriminated against Suzanne. She did not get the job, he said, because she was rude and did not have the right qualifications.

? question

1. Imagine you are the head of the employment tribunal in this case. What would your judgement be, and why? You should include the following:
   - Suzanne Jones applied for a job as . . .
   - She felt she did not get it because . . .
   - Mr Wheeler stated that Suzanne was not offered the job because . . .
   - In this case I think that Suzanne was/wasn't discriminated against because . . .

■ Yesterday and today

In the 1950s and 1960s some people feared that those coming from the Caribbean, India and Pakistan posed a threat to their jobs and housing. They faced a great deal of discrimination. For example, there were signs saying, 'Rooms to let – no coloureds'.

Racial discrimination of this kind, in employment and housing, became illegal in 1976.

? questions

2. List four reasons why people are racially prejudiced.

3. Is it right to have a law banning racial discrimination at work? Give reasons for your answer.

4. How do you think people like Mr Wheeler and Trevor's employers should be dealt with?

■ No joke

Trevor McCauley, from Northern Ireland, had worked in England for 20 years and had heard lots of jokes about the Irish. Over the last two years at work, however, he heard comments like this all the time.

He said they were saying things like 'typical thick Paddy'.

He complained and got the sack for being a troublemaker.

An employment tribunal decided that anti-Irish remarks amounted to racial discrimination and that Mr McCauley had been unfairly dismissed. He received £6,000 in compensation.

■ The law

Under the *Race Relations Act 1976*, it is against the law for an employer to treat people less well because of their race, colour, nationality or ethnic origin.

It is also against the law to discriminate against someone at work because of their religion or religious beliefs.

❖ keywords

Employment tribunal
A court of law that listens to cases brought by people who feel they have been unfairly sacked or badly treated at work.

Prejudice
Disliking people from a particular group because of their race, gender, sexuality, etc.

Racial discrimination
Treating people worse than others because of their race.

Looking for work

Race and unemployment

■ Looking for a solution

Damian Hannah is 22. He has eight GCSEs and two A levels. Two years ago he came to England from the West Indies. He wants to go to university but needs enough money first.

The only jobs he has managed to get so far are:

- stacking shelves in a supermarket
- working in a fast-food restaurant
- a cleaning job.

'I've been looking for some kind of office work,' said Damian. 'But they all ask for experience.

'I don't know if it's because of my colour. You see some black people doing really well, but I think it can make a difference where you live.

'I live in an area well known for violent crime and selling drugs. I think employers are put off when they see the postcode on my application form.'

Source: Labour Force Survey 2001

Table 1 Unemployment rates by ethnic origin, age and sex (per cent)

Age group	WOMEN		MEN	
	White	Ethnic minority groups	White	Ethnic minority groups
All	5	12	6	13
16–24 years	10	23	13	26
25–34 years	5	11	6	11
35–59/64 years	3	9	5	11

Source: Labour Force Survey 2001

Table 2 Unemployment rates by ethnic origin, education qualifications and sex (per cent)

Age group	WOMEN		MEN	
	White	Ethnic minority groups	White	Ethnic minority groups
Above A level	2	7	3	6
Up to and including A level	5	14	6	15
No qualifications	8	16	14	21

? questions

1. Damian isn't sure whether the colour of his skin is the reason he is unemployed. Look at Table 1. Now complete a speech bubble of what you might say to Damian. For example:

> Damian, I think that _____
> The evidence for this is _____

2. Damian asks whether unemployment rates are higher for people from ethnic minorities with good qualifications. Look at Table 2. Write a new bubble to explain.

3. What do you think are the effects of racial discrimination at work?

Reducing racial discrimination at work

Here are some things that the government could do to reduce racial discrimination at work.

Greater penalties Make firms or businesses who discriminate pay larger amounts in compensation.

Training Help workers to understand race issues more clearly.

Money Charge lower tax rates for companies who employ people from ethnic minorities.

Records Make all businesses above a certain size keep records of the ethnic origins of their employees, and publish these like school league tables.

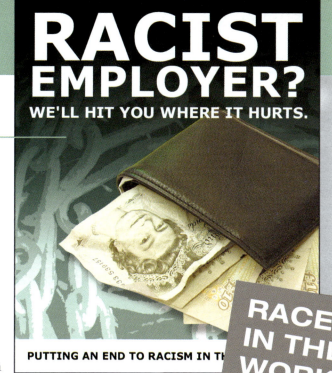

RACIST
EMPLOYER?
WE'LL HIT YOU WHERE IT HURTS.

PUTTING AN END TO RACISM IN TH

RACE ISSUES IN THE WORKPLACE

Training Day on July 26th

LOWER TAX

TAX REDUCTION
INCENTIVE FOR
ORGANISATIONS
TO EMPLOY MORE
WORKERS FROM
ETHNIC MINORITIES

THE GOVERNMENT yesterday announced that it is considering reducing tax rates for companies that employ more than an average number of workers from ethnic minorities.

In a move to get employers to take on

need for more people should have been tax incentive for Some say that if lower figures in general rates. When asked if saying such ideas can

? questions

4. Take two of the ideas for reducing racial discrimination from the list above. State what you think are the good and bad points about each one.

5. Make a poster that could be used by the government and sent to employers about how they could reduce racial discrimination.

Looking for work

Equal opportunities

■ Car crazy

Karen had always liked cars. She really wanted to be a mechanic.

In her final year at school, she saw an advert for two apprentice mechanics at a local garage. The salary was £7,000 a year. Karen had GCSEs in maths and science. She had done work experience in the garage.

At the interview, she was asked why she wanted the job and whether she thought she would fit in. She was also asked whether she minded getting her hands dirty.

Karen learnt that she was the best qualified of all the applicants. She stood a good chance of getting one of the jobs.

Two days later, Karen was told she had been turned down. Two 16-year-old boys had got the jobs instead.

Karen felt she had been a victim of **sex discrimination**. She decided to take her case to an employment tribunal.

? questions

1. You are the person making the judgement at Karen's tribunal. Sum up the case and then say what your decision is and why.
   - This case is about . . .
   - The questions Karen was asked at the interview were fair/unfair because . . .
   - My decision is that Karen has/has not been the victim of sex discrimination because . . .
   - She should/should not be compensated the sum of . . .
   - I have come to this figure based on . . .

2. Suggest two ways in which sex discrimination can take place in the workplace.

3. Explain what an employment tribunal is.

■ Boys, too

Sarat Sharma applied for a job as an office junior.

The letter inviting Sarat for interview began, 'Dear Miss Sharma'. When Sarat rang to say he would attend, the person he spoke to said that they were looking for a young female – and that Sarat would not be suitable.

Sarat's careers officer told him to report the

company for sex discrimination. With the help of the **Equal Opportunities Commission**, Sarat received £4,000 in compensation.

■ Stereotypes

Karen and Sarat were looking for jobs that people of their sex do not usually do. In doing so they were breaking the image of what men and women do – the stereotype.

Engineering apprenticeships

96% men

4% women

Health and social care apprenticeships

11% men

89% women

Computer analysts

79% men

21% women

Nursery and primary school teachers

14% men

86% women

? questions

4. Why do you think more men than women work as computer analysts or engineers? Why do more women than men work as nurses?

5. Does it matter if most car mechanics are men or most hospital nurses are women?

■ The law

The *Sex Discrimination Act 1975* says it is against the law for an employer to discriminate against job applicants because of their sex or because they are married or single.

However, the law does allow employers to discriminate in favour of women or men for reasons of decency, privacy or reality – for example, by choosing a male actor for a male role in a play.

Hi I'm your waitress

❖ keywords

Equal Opportunities Commission
An organisation working to get rid of sex discrimination. It is able to help and advise people who feel they have been unfairly treated because of their sex.

Sex discrimination
Treating someone less favourably because of their sex.

Looking for work

■ Train departure

Gemma worked as a train driver. She left her job when the company decided to change drivers' working hours. This required Gemma to work at any time. It meant that she could no longer be sure of being at home with her nine-year-old daughter in the evening or at weekends.

Gemma felt that this was unfair because it made life difficult for single parents – most of

whom were women. Gemma viewed this as unfair sex discrimination. She took her case to an employment tribunal.

The tribunal agreed with Gemma. They said that the company's new working arrangements were unfair to women.

This is known in law as indirect discrimination.

■ Direct and indirect discrimination

Direct discrimination takes place when someone is treated less well because of their sex, race or disability. Karen and Sarat (see pages 40–1) are examples of this.

Indirect discrimination happens when a situation or condition is imposed that discriminates unfairly against a particular sex, race or group of people, as in Gemma's case.

? question

1. Divide your page into 'direct' and 'indirect' discrimination. Put each case below in the correct column.

Judy started her new job. During her second week she wore trousers. She was asked to go home and change. The company did not allow women to wear trousers at work.

Neil was asked at his interview whether he would cut off his ponytail if he was given the job. He said no. His interview ended straightaway.

Linda, aged 31, could not apply for a job with the local council. The advert said that they wanted people aged between 18 and 28.

Nathan wanted to spend more time with his daughter. He asked his employer if he could go part-time like some female employees with children. The company refused.

Rhianna decided to leave her job after her boss kept putting his arm round her.

Equal pay

1971	Women's average full-time earnings 69% of men
2002	Women's average full-time earnings 82% of men

Top of the form Recent studies show that girls get better results at school and university than boys. But at work the situation is different.

Closing the gap? In 1971 women's average full-time earnings were 69 per cent of those of men.

By 2003 women's average full-time earnings were still less than those of men.

Who's the boss? In 2001, only 18 per cent of managers and directors were women.

Who's the Daddy?

? questions

2. Why do you think there are still differences in men's and women's pay? Give reasons.

3. Imagine that we have moved into the 2030s. Which of the following situations would you prefer? Explain why.

• **As we were**

Life has moved back to the 1930s when most married women stayed at home looking after the family.

• **Women on top**

Women's wages are now, on average, 20 per cent more than men's.

• **All on merit**

At work it makes no difference whether someone is a man or a woman. Pay and promotion depend upon how well they do their job.

• **No change**

The same as now. Some women do very well, but, on average, men earn more than women.

The law

Under the *Equal Pay Act 1970*, women and men should get the same wages and benefits (such as holidays and pensions) if they are doing like (similar) work or work of equal value.

Work of equal value means the work may be different, but is of equal skill. For example, a court decided that carpenters, painters and cooks who worked for a shipyard all had work of equal value.

Looking for work

Disability and beyond

■ A problem made worse

- Peter books a table in a restaurant. One member of the group has a guide dog. The manager says it will have to stay outside.

- Some taxi drivers refuse to let Durrand, a wheelchair user, in their cabs. They say that there is no room for his wheelchair.

- Caroline takes her brother, James, to a bar. James has learning difficulties. Caroline is told that her brother will put off other customers. They are asked not to come back.

The law also says that employers must make any reasonable changes to the workplace that would make it easier for a person with a disability to work there. For example:

- providing a special keyboard to help them use a computer
- giving them extra training
- rearranging where they might work.

The law applies to all organisations where there are 15 or more employees.

■ Discrimination at work

The *Disability Discrimination Act 1995* says it is against the law for an employer to treat a person with a disability worse than someone else, unless the person is:

- unsuitable for the work
- less suitable than the person who was given the job.

? questions

1. Pick one of the three cases below that you think is really unfair. Imagine you are the person involved. Write a diary entry for the day this happened, explaining what went on and how you feel about it.

   Will is a wheelchair user. He applies to work for a small firm of designers. He is well qualified for the job, but is turned down. It is felt that he would find it very difficult to get to the office, which is at the top of a spiral staircase with no access by lift.

   Paul is manager of a supermarket. He has worked for the company for several years. A year ago, Paul discovered that he was HIV-positive. He decides to tell his employer. The company worries that sales will suffer if the public hears of his illness. Paul is dismissed.

   David applies for a job collecting trolleys in a supermarket car park. From David's application form, the manager sees that David had attended a special school. He assumes that David has learning difficulties. David is not called for interview.

2. Should people have to retire at a certain age? Copy and complete the table below.

   Retirement at 65?

For	Against

3. Try to find a real case where someone felt they had been discriminated against because of their sex, race, disability or age. Summarise the case and say why the case is important.

■ Age discrimination

As they get older, many people face discrimination at work because of their age. This is not against the law, but it could change by 2005.

Too old Yvonne West, aged 46, applied for the post of deputy head. Although qualified for the job, she was not interviewed, because the head teacher and governors thought the job should go to someone under 40.

■ Other discrimination

Discriminating against someone at work because of their sexuality is not against the law (except for religious employers).

Sexuality Paul left his job as a barman after repeated abuse from his colleagues when they learnt that he was gay.

Working for a living

This unit looks at the legal rights and responsibilities of employers and employees.

In work

Anit is 17 and still at school. He is looking for a part-time job. He sees an advert in the window of a restaurant and goes in and asks to speak to someone about the job. Anit is asked to come back for an interview tomorrow.

? questions

1. What questions do you think Anit might be asked?

2. How do you think Anit should behave in his interview?

■ Interview

Anit is interviewed by Mr Bonner, the owner. He is asked why he has applied for the job and whether he has ever done similar work.

Anit says that he thinks the work would be interesting, but he has never worked in a restaurant before.

■ Offer

Mr Bonner tells Anit that he would:

- have to work on Saturdays and Sundays
- be paid £3.40 an hour
- have to work a four-hour shift
- have to wear a uniform of black trousers, orange shirt and black shoes, which he would have to provide himself
- have to wait on the tables
- have to help to keep the restaurant clean and tidy.

Anit is offered the job – and accepts.

? question

3. What questions do you think Anit should ask the owner of the restaurant?

■ Contract

In agreeing to take the job, Anit made a contract with Mr Bonner. A contract of employment is a legal agreement. It covers pay, hours and the nature of the job. In law these are known as 'express terms' – certain things about the job that both sides have agreed.

■ Training

Two days later, Anit begins his first evening at work. Hygiene rules for handling and storing food are explained to him.

Anit is shown:

- how to carry several plates of food to a table
- how to serve food
- how to keep a record of customer orders.

■ Rights and duties

As well as what is agreed in a contract, employers and employees have other rights and duties. Both sides expect these will be taken for granted. These are known as the 'implied terms' of a contract.

Mr Bonner, for example, must provide Anit with safe working conditions. Anit has a duty not to damage Mr Bonner's business. For example, he would be breaking his contract if he let a friend eat at the restaurant for half-price.

■ Written details

The law states that within two months of starting work, employees should be given a written statement of the terms and conditions of their work.

This should include details of:

- their starting date
- rate of pay
- hours of work
- holiday arrangements
- sick pay and pension
- the amount of notice that they and their employer must give if the contract is ended.

? questions

3. Draw up a list of the kinds of problems you think Anit might face while he is working at the restaurant.

4. Draw up Anit's contract.

Employment Contract

- E.g. hours of work
- uniform
- duties
- wages

Working for a living

A working life

■ Pay

Almost everyone in work is entitled to a pay slip saying:

- what they have been paid
- how it has been worked out.

In general, an employer is not allowed to take money from an employee's wage unless the employee agrees to it. However, they can take tax or national insurance, or take back money from someone who has been overpaid.

■ Minimum wage

The United Kingdom has a minimum wage. In October 2004 the government plans to introduce a minimum wage for people aged 16 and 17. It also plans to raise the minimum wage for 18–21 year olds from £3.80 to £4.10, and from £4.50 to £4.85 for over-21s.

? questions

Pay Anit's hourly rate is less than the national minimum wage.

Mistake At the end of the evening, the till is down by £15. A customer left without paying at one of Anit's tables. He is told that the money will be taken from his pay.

1. Anit comes to you for advice on these two situations. What would you tell him in each case?

2. Why do young people tend to get paid less than older workers? Is this fair? Is it fair if they are doing the same job?

Until then, there is no minimum wage for people under 18.

It is a criminal offence for an employer to pay below the minimum wage.

■ Health and safety

The *Health and Safety at Work Act 1974* states employers must take care of the safety of their staff.

This means they must provide:

- proper training
- safe equipment.

In an organisation with five or more employees, health and safety arrangements must be given to each employee in writing. Anyone injured at work should report the matter to their manager and get legal advice from their trade union or a solicitor.

■ Contract

Contracts of employment are important because they set out employees' rights. A contract – whether written down or oral – sets out the kind of job the employee will do, their hours, pay, holidays and the kinds of things for which they can be told off for.

Part-time workers It is against the law to discriminate against workers employed part-time. This means that part-timers should receive the same:

- rate of pay
- training
- holiday allowances.

? questions

3. Anit did not receive a written contract. Is he still protected by employment law? Explain your answer.

4. Look at the cases below. For each one say whether Anit's boss was right or wrong and why.

   The wrong shoes Anit comes to work in trainers. Mr Bonner sends him home. When he returns with the right shoes, Anit is told he must work an extra hour – the amount of time that he lost in collecting the shoes.

   No work If the restaurant is quiet Anit is sometimes sent home early. This means that on some shifts he gets only two hours' pay.

   Jobs At the start of each shift, Anit is often told to mop out the men's toilets. He feels this is unfair. He is employed as a waiter, not a cleaner.

   Hours When Anit works in the evening he has to stay until the last customer leaves. Sometimes he is unable to get away until after 11 p.m.

   Holiday Anit asks if is entitled to any holiday. Mr Bonner explains that he can take a week off but, unlike the other staff, he won't be paid, because he works only part-time.

Trade unions

This unit looks at the role of trade unions today.

Working hours

Home or away?

Yolanda's dad is a lorry driver. Her mum is a teacher. Her dad is often away from home. Sometimes Yolanda does not see him for two or three days at a time.

Yolanda and her mum do not spend much time together in the week. Her mum leaves for work at about 7.30 a.m. She gets home around 6 p.m. She has to mark or prepare work most evenings.

More, not less

A 2002 survey of 2200 children, aged 11–18, reported that one in five felt that their parents were too stressed to make time for them.

Other research in 2001 found that 61 per cent of working families have parents who work during the early morning, the evening or at weekends.

Employees can agree to work longer than this, but employers cannot make them do this.

In 2001, it was found that almost 4 million people in Britain work longer than 48 hours a week.

A nation of workers

The average working week in Britain is 43.6 hours.

One man in every ten works for more than 55 hours a week.

Working time

In 1998, the government adopted the European Working Time Directive and set a maximum working week of 48 hours.

Union challenge

In 1999, Britain's second largest trade union, Amicus, complained to the European Commission that the Working Time Directive was not being properly carried out.

The union was concerned that UK law did not make employers keep a record of extra hours that staff worked. The union felt that some workers felt under pressure to work longer.

Employers' organisations were against a change in the law. They said people should be able to choose how long they work and that limiting hours would reduce production.

51

Bill Morris, trade union leader

? question

1. • Children feel ignored because parents are working
   • People in Britain work long hours
   • Unions try to limit hours, but employers are against this.

   Pick one of the statements above and write a short speech to be given at a trade union meeting. Use this frame to help you.
   • I think that . . .
   • I believe this because . . .
   • My evidence for this is . . .
   • I would like to summarise my argument by . . .

■ A changing role

Beginning Trade unions first appeared in the eighteenth century. They were formed to help workers get better wages.

By the 1900s almost half of all the workers in Britain belonged to a union. During the Second World War (1939–1945) industry and unions worked closely together.

Change In the 1960s and 1970s, Britain had many industrial disputes. The unions were blamed. During the 1980s the Conservative government passed laws to weaken the trade unions, such as having to have a secret vote before strikes.

Now Union membership is going up. The role of unions has changed. It is less about pay deals, more about helping workers claim their legal rights.

? questions

2. Put the heading 'Trade unions' and complete the four headed boxes.

Late 18th century – unions began	1939–45	1960s–1970s	1980s

3. Ask your teacher/parents if they are in a union, which it is and why they made that choice. Report back to the class.

4. Your friend has just started working and asks you whether you think they should join a trade union. What is your advice?

5. Explain in your own words what a trade union is.

Losing your job

This unit looks at the law about dismissal from work.

Fired!

For three years Graham worked as a van driver for a printer. His boss was often unhappy with his work. He thought Graham was too slow.

One morning, Graham was running late. In trying to make up time he was caught speeding by a speed camera.

The company got a speeding penalty. Details were checked and it was clear that Graham had been driving the van. He was called into the manager's office and told that he needed to find another job. He was given three weeks' notice to leave.

> I DON'T BELIEVE IT! I'M LOST AND I'M LATE! WHAT CAN I DO?

> I'M NOT INTERESTED IN EXCUSES! YOU'RE FIRED!

■ Notice

 Finishing work When someone wants to leave their job, they must tell their employer, in advance, that they want to leave. This is normally set out in their terms and conditions of work.

If there is no written statement, someone who has worked for an employer for four weeks or more has to give seven days' notice.

Sacked An employee's terms and conditions will usually give the length of notice to which they are entitled.

If there is no written statement, the law says:

- After four weeks' work, one week's notice
- After two years' work, one week for each year
- After twelve years' work, twelve weeks. This is the most that can be given.
- An employer who does not give proper notice can be sued for wrongful dismissal.

? question

1. Graham's boss has to write a short report of what has happened. Write this report. You must include:
   • the job Graham did
   • his past record
   • the incident
   • your action.

▪ Instant dismissal

If an employee does something seriously wrong at work, their employer may decide to sack them on the spot.

Instant dismissal means that the employee loses the right to notice. They should have had the chance to defend themselves before the dismissal happens.

Serious misbehaviour (gross misconduct) includes theft, violence, dishonesty and damage to the employer's property.

▪ Go!

Claire worked as an office manager. She was instantly dismissed after her boss found out that she had been arranging her holiday during working hours. For several days, Claire had been surfing the Internet looking for cheap holidays.

Claire said that she had been doing this only during her lunch breaks. She said she had spent less than two hours in all searching for a holiday.

Her boss reminded Claire that the company had written to all employees saying that office computers were not for personal use. Claire was told to leave immediately. Claire felt that her dismissal was unfair and took her claim to an employment tribunal.

? question

2. You have to make the judgement in Claire's case. Was she guilty of gross misconduct?
   • sum up the case
   • give your judgement
   • say why you have made this judgement.

Losing your job

Claiming unfair dismissal

■ Fair or unfair?

In this section, you will be asked to decide whether you think people have been dismissed from their job fairly or unfairly. But, before you do that, have a think about what makes a dismissal fair or unfair and complete the following sentences:

- A person is dismissed fairly when . . .
- A person is dismissed unfairly when . . .

■ Greater rights

Until 1971, employers were able to dismiss staff as they pleased. They just had to:

- give the correct notice
- pay the employee the money due to them.

Today, employees have much more protection against dismissal.

? question

1. Copy and complete the table below by deciding in each case whether you think the dismissal was fair or unfair.

Case	Fair	Unfair	Reason

Colette had been a secretary for two months. She was given the sack after taking a two-hour lunch break. She had been warned before about her poor timekeeping.

Martine lost her job in a bank, where she had worked for two years. Her boss found out that she had lied at her interview about having criminal convictions. She had been found guilty of theft three years before.

John had worked for the ambulance service for ten years. He lost his job after he injured his back lifting a heavy patient. He was dismissed because he could no longer do the same kind of work.

■ The law

Anyone who feels they have been unfairly dismissed, and have been working for their employer for a year,

may try to get compensation by taking the case to an employment tribunal. The tribunal can order that the employee be given their job back – but this is not usually done.

An employer must show that they had a fair reason for sacking the employee.

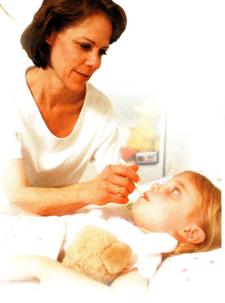

Fair The *Employment Rights Act 1996* says fair reasons for dismissal are:

- theft, fighting
- lateness all the time
- being unable to do the job
- redundancy (the job is no longer needed)
- so as not to break the law, for example a van driver loses his or her licence for drink-driving
- any other good reason.

Unfair Unfair reasons include:

- belonging to a trade union
- being pregnant
- being concerned about health and safety
- family emergencies.

Warnings If a worker is sacked for something small without warning, they may be able to sue for unfair dismissal. However, there is no law saying that warnings must be given before a person is sacked.

Dean had worked for three years in a sports shop. He was told that he would be losing his job because profits were down. A week after he had left, Dean noticed that someone else had been employed in his place.

Natasha made several mistakes during her first week as a cashier. Just before she went home on the Saturday, she was told that she was unsuitable, and was dismissed.

Losing your job

The employment tribunal

■ Reason to leave?

One morning, Kirsty Brennan received a call at work from her son's school to say he was ill. The school felt he ought to see a doctor.

Kirsty went to her boss, Mr Collier. She told him that her son was unwell and that she had to collect him from school. As she was leaving, Kirsty was told that Mr Collier had given her the sack.

Kirsty felt that she had been sacked unfairly. She decided to take her case to an employment tribunal.

At the tribunal Mr Collier said that Kirsty was rude. He said, 'She would fling files onto my desk. If I asked her to make any changes, she would snatch the paper and storm out.

'She did not ask if she could pick up her son,' he went on. 'She just told me she was leaving. She had only been here six weeks. This was the second time she needed time off.'

Kirsty said that she didn't have the chance to tell Mr Collier that she would return as soon as she had taken her son to the doctor.

? question

1. You have to make the decision at the tribunal. Was Kirsty unfairly dismissed? List the reasons which suggest that Kirsty was sacked unfairly and those which suggest she was not, and then make your decision.

■ A court of law

An employment tribunal is a special court dealing with employment disputes.

■ Procedure

Anyone claiming unfair dismissal must fill in a special form to set out details of their case.

It is important to get help with this from someone with experience. This could be a solicitor, someone from the Citizens' Advice Bureau or a trade union representative.

■ Paperwork

A lot of preparation is needed in gathering evidence. Often both sides have to let each other see all the evidence.

■ Finding a solution

One more attempt is made to help both sides reach agreement, and avoid going to court. Often this is successful.

At the tribunal

Tribunals are more informal than other courts of law. No one wears a gown or a wig.

The panel has three people:

- a legally qualified chairperson.
- one person who is an employer.
- another who works for a trade union.

There should be at least one man and one woman on the panel

The decision

The tribunal usually orders compensation to be paid if it agrees that the employee has been unfairly dismissed.

Tribunals are allowed to order that the employee should be given their job back – but rarely do.

The cost

The average cost of taking a case to a tribunal is £2,000 in fees and time.

If the employee wins, he or she is often worse off. The average award is under £3,000. More than half the people who take their cases to tribunals are in lower-paid jobs afterwards.

? question

2. You work for the Citizens Advice Bureau. Put instructions on your web page about what people should do if they feel they have been unfairly dismissed. The web page should include:

- a suitable headline
- the first step
- whom people would ask to help them
- what happens at the employment tribunal.

✳ coursework idea

Try to find a case that went to an employment tribunal reported in two newspapers.
- put in your own words what each article says
- put in the background (the law, how tribunals work)
- say how each side sees it and why
- say what your view is and why
- say why your view might be different from other people's.

Unequal Britain

This unit looks at inequalities in Britain today and efforts that are being made to bring them to an end.

Racism

■ Battered to death

At the beginning of 2000 Zahid Mubarek, aged 19, was sentenced to 90 days in a **Young Offenders Institution**. He had broken into a car and taken razor blades worth £6.

Near the end of his sentence he was put in a cell with Robert Stewart, aged 20, who was thought to be dangerous and disturbed. He had been charged with sending racist hate mail. Letters home referred to the numbers of 'niggers on the wing'.

Robert Stewart battered Zahid to death using a table leg. After the death of his son, Mr Mubarek said, 'There was always a lot of racist abuse going on. The prison warders let it happen.'

? question

1. Write a newspaper report about this story. These words and phrases will help you:

> Zahid Mubarek
> petty offence
> Young Offenders Institution
> Robert Stewart
> disturbed
> racist
> battered
> responsibility

Racial equality is an important issue, for both staff and prisoners

■ Racism in prison

An investigation took place into the running of the Young Offenders Institution. It found that the behaviour of a small number of officers was openly racist. Asian and black prisoners were twice as likely to be separated from other prisoners, and have restraint used against them.

Another investigation in another prison reported that of the Asian prisoners questioned:

- 49 per cent had been racially abused
- 12 per cent said that they had been attacked.

■ Institutionalised racism

Institutionalised racism occurs when an organisation fails to give people a proper service because of their colour, culture or ethnic origin. It can involve prejudice, ignorance or stereotyping.

COMMISSION FOR RACIAL EQUALITY

Second-class citizen Farouk Stemmet caught the train from Liverpool to Sunderland and headed for the first-class carriage. He was stopped by the conductor and told to sit somewhere else. Mr Stemmet explained that he had a first-class ticket. When the conductor checked the ticket, Mr Stemmet protested about the way he had been treated. The conductor claimed that he was only doing his job. He said that Mr Stemmet had a chip on his shoulder because he was black.

Mr Stemmet made a complaint to the rail company and reported the matter to the **Commission for Racial Equality** (CRE).

? questions

2. Tell the story using speech bubbles. The first one has been done for you.

> Where are you going? This is first-class.

| Conductor | Mr Stemmet |

3. Why do you think the conductor behaved as he did?

4. How do you think the rail company should deal with Mr Stemmet's complaint? For example, do you think they should:
   - send Mr Stemmet a letter of apology?
   - offer to pay him compensation?
   - dismiss the conductor?
   - give all conductors training so that they don't make the same mistake?
   - do nothing at all?

■ The law

The *Race Relations Act 1976* says it is unlawful to discriminate against anyone on the grounds of race, colour, nationality, religion or ethnic origin.

❖ keywords

Young Offenders Institution
Place where young offenders, aged 15–21, are held in custody.

Commission for Racial Equality (CRE)
A national organisation giving help and advice to people who believe they have suffered race discrimination. It is also able to take action itself against an employer who breaks race discrimination laws.

Unequal Britain

Separate or together?

After the riots in 2001, Oldham and Burnley (below).

■ Trouble on the streets

Between April and June 2001 several towns in the north of England suffered from street rioting. The trouble took place between white and Asian young people, in areas where unemployment is high and housing is poor.

One of those towns was Oldham in Lancashire where 11 per cent of the population are British Asian. Most people of Asian background in Oldham live close together in the poorest areas. They are more likely to be unemployed than white people. Over the years districts of the town have divided along racial lines. Schools have become either mainly white or Asian.

In a report on the riots, Oldham Council was criticised for not doing enough to prevent this division.

■ Parallel lives

Where there is little understanding between different groups of people fear and suspicion can grow.

In Burnley there were also riots:

- fights took place between Asian and white drug gangs
- an Asian taxi driver was attacked with a hammer

- bricks were thrown through a pub window by Asian men – they believed people in there were planning to attack them
- Asian businesses were attacked.

? question

1. At the time of the riots in 2001 British Asian and white communities in Oldham were completely separate. Write down a list of problems that this might cause. The words listed below might help you with this:

fear	prejudice
ignorance	schools
separation	gangs
housing	

It was thought that, as in Oldham, there were not many chances for Asian and white people to mix together.

Peace making

The report into the riots said these things would help stop further trouble:

- *Housing* Make housing estates racially mixed.
- *Jobs* Make more jobs so that people are better off and less likely to listen to racist arguments.
- *Schools* Change catchment areas to make schools more racially and religiously mixed.
- *Councils* Have more council workers from ethnic minorities.
- *Democracy* Listen to what people say and encourage more people to get involved.

? question

2. You are at a council meeting. Put the suggestions of the report (opposite) in the order you would deal with them. Explain why.

A sense of belonging

In a speech after the riots, the Home Secretary, David Blunkett, said that problems were more likely to happen where newcomers and their families did not speak English. This, he said, made it difficult for people to mix and become part of the main community.

Mr Blunkett added that learning English did not mean that anyone would have to give up their own way of life.

It seems that all the young people who took part in the riots could speak English perfectly.

? questions

3. Do you think that not speaking English stops communities mixing, or are there other reasons?

4. Suggest three things that help people get along well together where they live.

Unequal Britain

Sexual equality

■ Aiming high

Rosie is 15 and has everything to live for. She is clever, with lots of friends and a cheerful personality. Her hobbies are gymnastics and football, and she is very good at both.

One day she hopes to represent her country at one of these sports. Rosie would like to be a lawyer and perhaps a judge. She'd also like to do something that helps people, which is why she thinks that she could one day become an MP.

All the statistics opposite obtained from the Equal Opportunities Commission

? question

1. How likely is it that Rosie will achieve her ambitions? Give reasons.

■ Life chances

Education Qualifications play a large part in the job you will get. Men as a whole have better qualifications than women. Young women have better qualifications than men at that age.

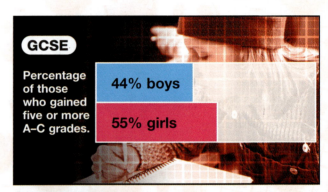

GCSE

Percentage of those who gained five or more A–C grades.

44% boys

55% girls

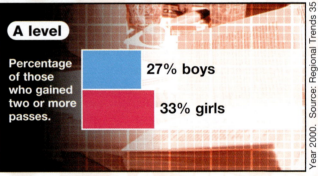

A level

Percentage of those who gained two or more passes.

27% boys

33% girls

Year 2000. Source: Regional Trends 35

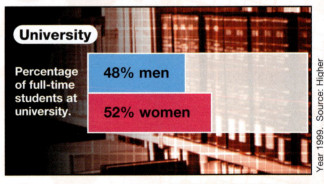

University

Percentage of full-time students at university.

48% men

52% women

Year 1999. Source: Higher Education Statistics Agency

★ fact

It was not until 1895 that women were able to get a degree at most British universities. Oxford allowed this in 1920 and Cambridge in 1948.

Employment by occupation 2000

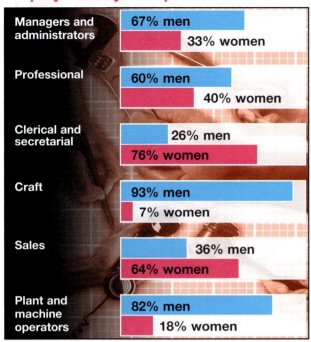

	Men	Women
Managers and administrators	67% men	33% women
Professional	60% men	40% women
Clerical and secretarial	26% men	76% women
Craft	93% men	7% women
Sales	36% men	64% women
Plant and machine operators	82% men	18% women

Source: Office for National Statistics

* fact

The first woman MP who actually sat in Parliament was Nancy Astor, MP for Plymouth Sutton in Devon, in 1919.

? questions

2. Study the tables on education and work. What do you notice about girls' achievement at GCSE, A level and university?

3. Now look at the table on work. Do men or women have the top jobs? Why does this seem strange when you look at the education tables?

4. What do you notice about the jobs that men and women do?

* facts

Married women did not start remaining at home to look after children until the nineteenth century. Until then women did farm work and worked as butchers, printers, carpenters, brewers and blacksmiths.

The hourly earnings of women working full time are on average 82 per cent of those of men.

Politics

Source: Year 2001

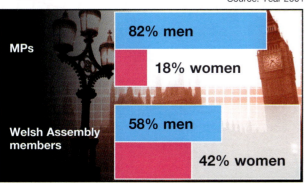

	Men	Women
MPs	82% men	18% women
Welsh Assembly members	58% men	42% women

■ The law

The *Sex Discrimination Act 1975* says it is against the law to treat a person less well because of their sex.

The *Equal Pay Act 1970* gives women the rights to equal pay and benefits for the same or similar work. Women should not lose their job because of pregnancy, childbirth or the care of their children.

Parents of children born after 14 December 1999 have the right to take up to 13 weeks unpaid leave during the first five years of their life.

Unequal Britain

The long struggle

Men's property

Before 1882, married women were not allowed to own property. Once they got married, everything they owned belonged to their husbands.

A man could divorce his wife, but it was almost impossible for a woman to divorce her husband. It wasn't until 1923 that divorce was available to both men and women.

In almost every part of life, men and women were treated unequally.

Campaigners

However, a few women were not happy with this situation. Somehow they needed to have the vote and get women into Parliament. By 1885 all men had been given the vote, but not women. No woman could stand for election as a Member of Parliament.

Women began to campaign for the vote. They were called 'suffragettes', from the word 'suffrage', meaning 'the right to vote'. By 1906 their leader, Emmeline Pankhurst, decided that more pressure was needed. They broke windows, damaged government buildings, and attacked MPs.

First World War 1914–18

The suffragettes stopped their campaign in 1914. They encouraged women to work for the war by going into industry or joining the armed services.

As the men were fighting, women did the work previously done by men. People began to feel women were more capable.

In 1918, women over 30 were given the vote. In 1928 it was given to women over 21.

Women in Parliament

Women were allowed to stand for Parliament in 1918. Only one was successful. Until 1987 there were no more than 30 women MPs in Parliament at any one time. After the 2001 election there were 118.

For and against

Here are two statements about positive discrimination – both made by women MPs, and both from the Conservative Party:

'We whinge and whine and demand special treatment. If that isn't an insult to women, I don't know what is.'
Ann Widdecombe MP

'There are many women not being selected who would make first-class MPs and Parliament is missing out on a pool of talent that would strengthen this house.'
Theresa May MP

Positive discrimination

Before the 1997 election, the Labour Party decided to try to get more women into Parliament. They did this by making sure that only women candidates stood in **safe seats**.

Some men who had wanted to stand for election felt this was unfair and took the matter to court. The court ruled that this kind of **'positive discrimination'** (treating a group better to help improve their unfair position) was against the law and unfairly discriminated against men.

? questions

1. Draw and complete a step diagram to show how women have come to play a greater part in politics, for example:

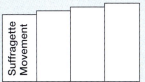

2. Write a short speech for the radio to say whether it matters that women make up more than half the population of the UK but have only 18 per cent of the MPs.

? questions

3. Do you think it is right to try to get more women into Parliament by making sure they are candidates in safe seats?

4. List two other groups of people who could be helped by positive discrimination.

keywords

Positive discrimination
Treating a group of people better than others.

Safe seats
Seats in Parliament that a party is sure to win.

Unequal Britain

Challenging disability

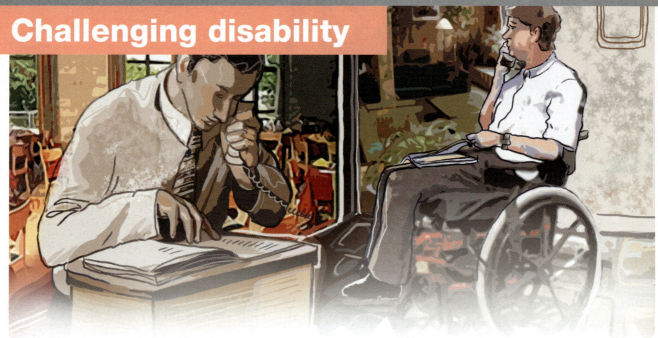

Dining out

Robert was looking forward to dinner with some friends. A table for seven was booked at a local restaurant.

One of his friends rang the restaurant to confirm the booking. He said that there would be one wheelchair user in the party – Robert.

The owner said he was sorry. The restaurant could not cater for wheelchair users. It would be too crowded. The friend was angry and cancelled the booking.

? questions

1. You have been asked by the local newspaper to cover this story. Think of a suitable headline.

2. The restaurant owner refused to allow Robert into the restaurant at a busy time. Do you think he was right or wrong to do this? Give reasons for your answer.

   The words and phrases below may help you:

overcrowding	fire
discrimination	safety
Robert's feelings	unfair

What is a disability?

Disability includes:

- needing to use a wheelchair
- blindness
- deafness
- learning difficulties
- mental illness
- brain damage from strokes or accidents.

There are 8.5 million people with some form of disability in Britain. That is about one person in seven.

Dependent on charity

In Victorian England many disabled children had to beg or steal for a living.

One man, John Groom, helped girls with disabilities. He gave them work making artificial flowers that could be sold on the streets and in shops. The money from the flowers and charitable donations helped pay for the girls to live in decent homes. They were looked after by specially trained nurses and housekeepers.

In 1866 John Groom founded his charity to care for disabled young women. Today, this and many other charities provide help and support for people with disabilities.

Rights, not charity

Charities play an important part in helping people. All charities are limited in the number of people they can help. For a long time people with disabilities, like Robert, were unable to do anything about the discrimination that they faced. This was why a new law was needed.

Disability Discrimination Act 1995

This Act says it is unlawful to treat someone less well because of a disability. This covers work and other areas of life, such as shopping, having a meal, or going to the doctor's.

Robert took his case to the Disability Rights Commission. This advises people of their rights. It helps them with legal cases. As a result of legal action, the restaurant owner apologised to Robert and agreed to pay him £200 in compensation. The restaurant owner was given advice on how he and his staff should treat customers with disabilities.

Education

In 2001 the *Special Educational Needs and Disability Act* made it unlawful to discriminate in the education of people with disabilities. Schools have a duty not to treat students less well because of their disability. They should make reasonable changes: for example, making sure disabled people can get to rooms where they have lessons. Schools do not have to change the buildings.

? question

3. Look at your own school. What problems does a person in a wheelchair face trying to attend your school?

Older people

This unit examines the lives of older people in the UK, and how they are seen and treated by others.

The future is grey

? questions

1. Which of these people in the photos to the right would you describe as old? Would it be all of them, or just one or two?

2. What makes you think of someone as being old?

3. Identify two good things about being old and two bad things.

■ Too old?

Winston Churchill In 1945, at the end of the Second World War, Sir Winston Churchill was 71. For the previous six years he had led Britain through the war. He was defeated in the 1945 general election, but returned as Prime Minister in 1951. He retired in 1955 at the age of 81.

Nelson Mandela
Nelson Mandela was also 81 when he retired as President of South Africa in 1999. In 1965 he was put in prison because of his political activities against apartheid (the separation of black and white people). In 1990 he was released. In 1994, at the age of 76, he was elected president.

■ One hundred and rising

People aged over 100 in Britain

Date	Number
1950	300
2003	6000
2036	40,000 (estimate)
2066	95,000 (estimate)

Life expectancy The average life expectancy in Britain is 75 years for a man and 79 for a woman. This is three more years than ten years ago. People over 65 now make up one-fifth of the population.

Research shows this is because we are avoiding some of the things that killed us in the past such as:

- poor living conditions
- poor diet . . .

. . . and because of new drugs and medical techniques. People are also smoking less.

Health Although people are living longer, many suffer from ill health. Two-thirds of people over 75 have a long-standing illness.

Change

We need to adapt to meet the needs of our ageing population. In the future there will be many more older people in Britain (and in other countries too). How should we deal with this? Here are some suggestions:

- spend more on housing, so that older people have somewhere comfortable to live
- provide extra education and leisure services, to help fill people's time
- make sure people have help in the home
- provide more medical services
- set aside more money for pensions
- provide better public transport.

? questions

5. What kind of things do older people give to society?

6. If the government could afford to spend money on only three of the points listed opposite, which would you choose? Explain why.

Priority	Reason
1. Pensions	

7. How much responsibility does the government have to help older people?

HIS **DAD'S** POPPING ROUND TO VISIT LATER ON...

Older people

An age-old problem

Wards A-C
X-ray Dept

■ Standards of care

It was a cold day in February. Two elderly patients, Edith Vance and Dorothy Gately, needed to have an X-ray. An ambulance was used to carry them from the ward to another building for the X-ray.

Neither patient was wearing a dressing gown or slippers. The blanket that they were each given did not cover their legs and feet.

A porter took the two patients in their wheelchairs from the ward. He pushed Edith ahead of him. Dorothy was towed behind. When they reached the ambulance, Edith was left in the road, while Dorothy was put onto the ambulance lift. When they reached the X-ray department, Edith again was left to wait.

While she waited, Edith asked what was happening. Neither the porter nor ambulance driver replied.

The porter wheeled both patients into the X-ray building. He used the footrest of the first wheelchair to push open the door. As they moved thorough the entrance, the door swung back hitting Edith, who was coming through backwards, on the back of the head.

While they waited for their X-ray, neither Dorothy nor Edith was told how long she would have to wait.

❓ questions

1. What was wrong with Edith's and Dorothy's treatment? List as many points as you can.

2. Why was it wrong?

3. What action do you think the hospital should take?

Rationing

Medical treatment is very expensive. No health service in the world can give every patient everything that they need.

Hospital staff have to make decisions about who will receive the treatment that is available. Sometimes they decide that this will be based on age.

Unfair? Charlie Hughes is 85 years old. He has a heart problem that could be helped by having surgery. Mr Hughes's GP sent him to see a specialist.

At the hospital, the surgeon said he couldn't understand why Mr Hughes was there. 'There are men in their fifties still able to work who need this operation,' he said. He added that, at his age, Mr Hughes had little chance of having this operation.

Mr Hughes said it would be much fairer if everyone, no matter what their age, put their name on a waiting list and received their treatment in turn.

Discrimination at work

The United States has a law that forbids age discrimination at work against anyone over 40. For example, if two people age 30 and 45 apply for a job, selecting the 30-year-old on grounds of age alone would be against the law.

In Britain we have a code of conduct for employers. It recommends that the workforce should cover a wide age range and that age limits should be avoided. The European Union has said that age discrimination should be reduced, but this is not yet law.

? question

6. 'Discrimination on grounds of age should be made illegal.'
   - give one argument agreeing with this
   - give one argument against this.

Which argument is stronger? Do you agree or disagree with the statement?

? questions

4. Do you agree with Charlie Hughes?

   'I agree/disagree that older people should have the same right to medical treatment as younger people because …'

5. A 17-year-old with cancer deserves to be treated ahead of somebody who is 70.

   'I agree/disagree with this statement because …'

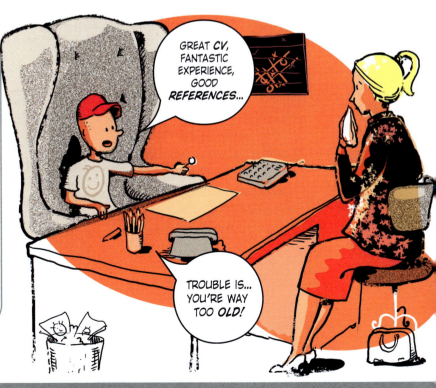

GREAT *CV*, FANTASTIC EXPERIENCE, GOOD *REFERENCES*…

TROUBLE IS… YOU'RE WAY TOO *OLD!*

Older people

Older but still active

■ Respect

In some communities, older people are treated with great respect. Their age has given them an experience and understanding that is valued in the community.

In the UK, however, it is often said that older people are not given the same respect as before. This does not mean that older people were always well looked after. In Victorian times, many ended their lives in a workhouse, where they did unpaid work for food and housing.

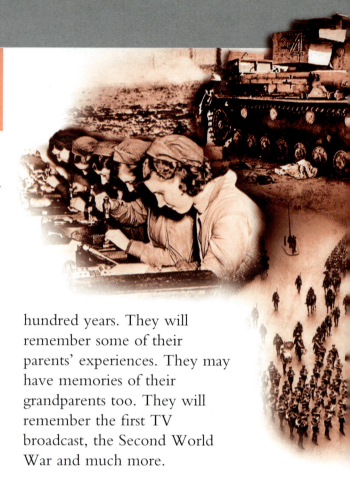

hundred years. They will remember some of their parents' experiences. They may have memories of their grandparents too. They will remember the first TV broadcast, the Second World War and much more.

? question

1. Write a short letter to a local newspaper as if you were an old person. You feel that you are either given little respect by society, or you are treated well.

   Dear Editor,

   I think that …
   I believe this is because …
   I would also argue that …
   My evidence for this is that …
   I also believe that …
   Therefore, I would like to sum up my argument by saying that …

   Yours sincerely

■ Fund of knowledge

A person aged 70 or 80 today may well have a memory that goes back more than a

? questions

2. Write five questions to ask to an older person about their memories.
   For example, 'What were your school days like?'
   You may like to record the interview and share with the class.

3. Identify two advantages of talking and listening to older people.

■ Living in the now

Many older people live life to the full, even though their bodies are slowing down. John Malyon, aged 68, says, 'I am an accountant by training. I didn't want to stop working, so I contacted a charity and the local football club. For ten years I have helped them both keep their financial records.'

? questions

4. Identify three types of voluntary work older people help with in your community.

5. What are the benefits to themselves and the people they help? Give an example.

6. Suggest and explain one way older people could get involved as volunteers in your school.

■ Campaigning

The Beth Johnson Foundation in Stoke-on-Trent is a charity that aims to improve the quality of life for older people.

One of its recent projects involved getting together with young people to campaign on issues that affect them both, such as burglary and the high cost of transport.

The project members came to understand each other better and in many cases became good friends.

■ Pensioners' union

In 1979 the National Pensioners' Convention was set up. It is a pressure group run *by* pensioners *for* pensioners. It organises meetings, rallies and demonstrations, gives advice and **lobbies** politicians.

keyword

Lobbying
Writing to or meeting MPs (and others in authority) in order to campaign for changes in the law.

✳ coursework ideas

1. Write about any voluntary work you have done with older people, or any fundraising you have done to help older people.
   These questions might help you:

   • What did you do?

   • How was it organised

   • Why did you do it?

   • What did you achieve?

   • What would you change if you did it again and why?

Refugees

This unit looks at the situation facing many refugees, especially those who come to Britain. It looks at the reasons they have left their country and what treatment they should receive.

Moving images

■ A sign of our times

- In 2001 about 23 million people were either refugees or moved out of their home or area within their own country.
- Most people who become refugees leave their home or country because everyday life is almost impossible, for example, Kosovo crisis of 1999 (see page 77).
- War in a country where most live in poverty makes the problem worse. Fighting stops the supply of food. People leave to escape famine and disease, for example, Somalia, 1990s.
- People can be refugees because they are picked on because of their ethnic or religious groups, for example, Jews, Kurds in Iraq and Turkey.

? questions

1. What feelings do you have as you look at these pictures?

2. What do these pictures show about the kind of problems that refugees most often face? What other difficulties might refugees face?

3. Why do people become refugees?

    Here are some words that may help you to answer:
    - war
    - poverty
    - discrimination
    - famine
    - persecution.

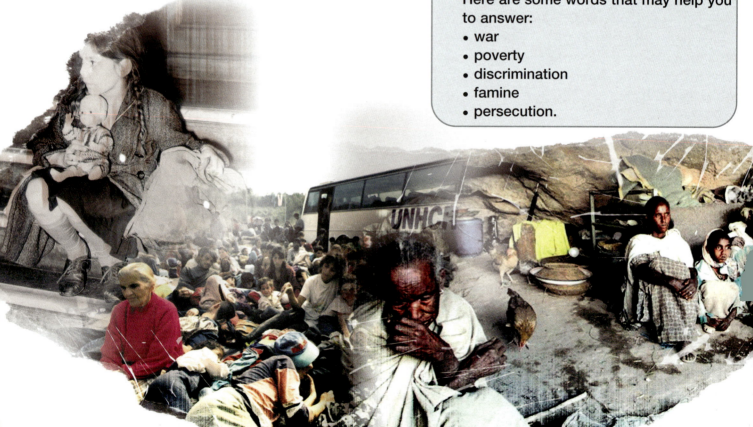

■ Leaving home

Lian Hu Su lived in Beijing, the capital of China. In 1989 students, workers and many others took part in demonstrations against the government. They thought that it should give people more freedom.

It was an offence to demonstrate against the government and to help anybody who was doing so. The army dealt with the protesters very severely.

Lian Hu Su felt the government was wrong. He hid some protesters in his home. He was reported to the government. As the police were on their way to his flat, Lian Hu Su escaped.

Michaela lived with her family in Romania. As a Roma Gypsy, she faced a lot of prejudice and discrimination. In 2002 she left Romania for a better life.

'Here you are very rich or very poor,' she said. 'My family, we have nothing. Everyone has the right to seek happiness.'

Michaela's family paid for her to travel from Romania to France hidden in a lorry. In Paris she hid under the carriage of a Eurostar train. She was discovered by the police at Waterloo Station in London.

Shukri Ebrahim lived with her family in Somalia, in northeast Africa. There had been fighting between the government and different groups. The government believed that Shukri's father was a member of one such group. One day three soldiers came to their house to take him away.

Shukri and her family were quite alone. They decided they had to leave.

? questions

4. Read the three stories on this page, and write down the reason why each person left their country.

5. Should anyone help the people in these cases? If so, who? Try to explain the reasons for your view.

Refugees

War and peace

Much of British history has been shaped by war and peace.

■ Invasion

From 55 BC to AD 1066, Britain was invaded by:

- Romans
- Angles and Saxons
- Vikings
- Normans.

■ Safety

Others have come to escape war. For example:

- merchants from Armenia (a country set between Russia and Iran) in the thirteenth century
- families from Kosovo in 1990.

★ facts

France Britain's reputation as a country offering safety to people who are being persecuted began with the arrival of the Huguenots from France. These were Protestants who were persecuted for their beliefs by the Roman Catholic Church in France, between 1560 and 1685. Thousands died, but about 150,000 people escaped to safety in England, Ireland and America.

Russia Jewish communities have lived in Russia for 2,000 years. During this time they have been persecuted there and in many other countries.

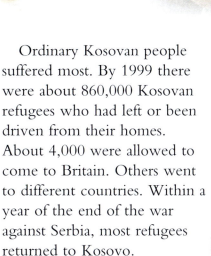

In 1835, the Czar (the ruler of Russia), ordered all the Jewish people to move to the western edge of the Russian empire. Jews were told where they could:

- live
- travel
- earn a living.

Jews were often blamed for crimes, which they almost always had not committed.

In 1881 Czar Alexander II was assassinated. One of those responsible was a Jewish woman. The result was an outbreak of violent attacks (called 'pogroms') on Jewish people in Russia.

Thousands of Jews were killed. Groups were organised by the government to break up homes and destroy businesses. The leaders of these groups were looked up to. For their own safety, many Jewish families started to leave.

■ Kosovo

The province of Kosovo used to be part of Yugoslavia, with local leaders having some control over their own affairs.

This all changed with the break-up of Yugoslavia. From 1989 the mainly Albanian Muslim population of Kosovo was ruled by Serbia. Most Kosovans believed they should be independent from Serbia. Most Serbs believed they should not.

Kosovans protested about the unequal ways in which they were treated. Some formed the Kosovan Liberation Army. They attacked and killed members of the Serbian forces in Kosovo.

The Serbian Government then killed many Kosovans. They tried to drive others out of the country. The European Union, the United States and other countries sent troops in to stop this.

Ordinary Kosovan people suffered most. By 1999 there were about 860,000 Kosovan refugees who had left or been driven from their homes. About 4,000 were allowed to come to Britain. Others went to different countries. Within a year of the end of the war against Serbia, most refugees returned to Kosovo.

Podrimad Xheudet aged 29

- a teacher in Kosovo
- in danger
- moved to Pristina, the capital
- moved again when the capital was attacked
- house and car burned
- father and brothers beaten

? question

1. Think of three or four questions you would want to ask someone who is a refugee.

Refugees

Permission to stay

■ Going back or staying on?

Many people who seek safety abroad eventually return to their own country. Those who wish to stay must apply for **asylum**.

When someone seeks asylum, they are asking to be accepted as a refugee. If they are successful they will be allowed to stay. If they are not, they will be sent back to their own country.

■ Refugee status

Deciding whether a person can stay in a country permanently is complicated. In simple terms, officials have to decide whether the person fits a certain definition of the word 'refugee'. This is set out in the United Nations Convention (1951). It can be summarised as follows:

refugee \Ref`u*gee"\ n.

A refugee is a person who is outside their country and cannot return because of a well-founded fear of persecution for reasons of race, religion, nationality, membership of a particular social group or political opinion.

Someone whose situation does not meet the above test may still be allowed to stay, and be given what is called Exceptional Leave to Remain. By special agreement they are allowed to stay in Britain if sending them home would seem to be very cruel or unkind.

■ Waiting for a decision

Refugees who are waiting for a decision about their asylum claim are known as 'asylum seekers'. Some have to wait years for a decision. The Government is now trying to speed up the process.

? question

1. You are the person who has to decide whether each of the following people should be allowed to stay. For two of the people copy and complete the table.

Name	
Problems	
Reasons asylum wanted	
My decision	
Reason for my decision	

Muna's brother was executed in 1990 for plotting to overthrow the government in Sudan. Muna helped form an organisation to support the families of those who had been killed by government forces. She was arrested many times.

She came to England to stay with friends. She then asked for asylum. She felt that she could not face the danger any more.

Milan is a Roma from Slovakia. He asked for asylum in Britain after being attacked many times in Slovakia. He said that there was a lot of prejudice against Roma people there. 'We have words like "Gypsies to the gas chamber" painted on our wall.'

The British Government recognises that Roma people do have difficulties in Slovakia, but believes that the police there do provide some protection.

Sadiq's father was a politician in Iraq. He criticised the government. One day, Sadiq was taken in for questioning. The soldiers wanted to know where his father was. He refused to tell them and was tortured. He was released but the questioning and beatings continued. Sadiq felt he had to leave and went to England.

Arif came to Britain as a refugee from Kosovo. While he was here, he became ill and was taken to hospital. Arif was told that he had a serious heart condition. He applied for asylum in Britain. He asked not to be returned to Kosovo, because there were no medical facilities there for his illness.

◆ keyword

Asylum
Seeking safety in another country when you are being persecuted for reasons of your race, religion, nationality, membership of a particular social group or political opinion.

Refugees

Modern times

■ Myth and reality

HANDOUT HUNTERS

We're allowing freeloaders into our small country when we have enough troubles with our anti-social elements. The asylum laws should be immediately changed to ensure that we are not flooded with no-good people scurrying around the world looking for handouts.

A Thompson, Truro, Cornwall.

ASYLUM CAMP

Should Britain keep taking immigrants? No, Britain does not have the space or money to take in the same number it allowed during the past 40 years. Walk in London and watch refugees thrusting babies at passers-by demanding money. I will not welcome other people here. We need a guarantee that if let in, refugees will be sent back when they can be and nobody will be accepted for political reasons.

J M Potton, Middlesex.

■ The big picture

Refugees in Britain The table below shows the numbers of people who asked for political asylum in Britain from 1998 to 2000. Some of those who asked in 1998 did not have their cases examined until 2000.

The waiting time is now getting much shorter.

Thirty-one per cent of the people who applied to the UK for asylum were allowed to stay in this country.

? questions

The letters above appeared in an English newspaper.

1. Look at 'Handout hunters'. List the words that show the writer is against refugees.

2. Look at 'Asylum camp'. Identify the two arguments against refugees.

3. Write a headline and three sentences to give the other side of the argument.

Refugees from Kosovo were taken to many parts of Britain. The banner over the door reads 'Welcome to Doncaster'.

Year	Numbers seeking asylum	Numbers granted asylum	Numbers allowed to stay temporarily	Numbers refused asylum
2000	80,315	10,375	11,495	72,015
1999	71,160	7,815	2,465	18,390
1998	46,015	5,345	3,910	22,315

Out of every 5,000 people in the UK, six are asylum seekers and one will be allowed to stay.

Other countries The world's poorest countries have the greatest number of refugees. For example:

- In 2001, Iran had 1.8 million refugees from Afghanistan
- In 2000 half a million people left Sierra Leone in West Africa for Guinea, Liberia and Gambia.

Between 1991 and 2000, Germany had 1.7 million applications for asylum. The UK received 428,000 applications over the same period.

However, in 2000, the UK received more asylum applications than any other country in Europe. But, as a percentage of a country's population, the UK is ninth on the list.

Costs The cost of dealing with applications has risen from £475 million in 1999 to £590 million in 2000. This is still less than a quarter of a per cent of the amount we spend on public spending.

Some people say that asylum seekers come to this country to get as much free support as possible. The rules state that asylum seekers:

- are not allowed to work in the first six months of their stay
- may be provided with approximately £35 a week.

The Government wants to encourage highly skilled people to settle in Britain.

In the past, many refugees have done a lot for our society. Examples include Albert Einstein, Sigmund Freud and Karl Marx.

Many people who seek asylum in Britain already have skills and qualifications, for example in engineering and science. When they are eventually allowed to work, they all make a contribution to our economy.

 **coursework idea**

Try to find two newspaper articles that deal with asylum seekers in a different way.

- summarise the articles
- say how they are different
- give your own view and why
- say why the issue is important.

Families

The first part of this unit looks at some of the different kinds of family in Britain today.

Changing times

■ Yesterday

Sheila and Patrick Callanan were married in 1953. They soon started a family and, over the next 18 years, had a total of 12 children. This was unusually large in the 1960s and 1970s. Sheila and Patrick were married for just over 35 years, until Patrick died in 1989.

■ Today

Four of the Callanan children still live in the family home. Eleven of them meet weekly for Sunday lunch, cooked by their mother.

■ Marriage

Six of the children have partners, five have married and three have children. Most have decided to stay single or not yet marry.

■ Traditional families: image or reality?

The Callanans are what is known as an extended family. More common is the nuclear family of two married parents living with their children at the same address, and often some distance from close relations. This is just one example of the different forms of family pattern that we have today.

? question

1. Look at all the information on this page about changing families and draw two storyboards/diagrams to show the family in the past and now. For example:

   'Families in the past'

   Families were large and close

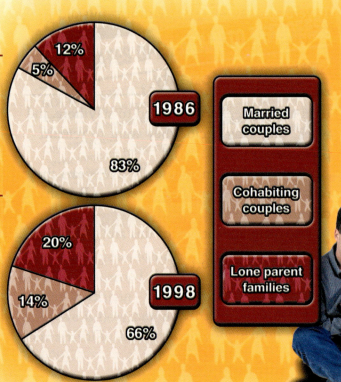

12%
5%
1986
83%

Married couples

Cohabiting couples

Lone parent families

20%
14%
1998
66%

Explaining family diversity

Family patterns today can vary a great deal. They may be:

- one-parent families
- living together but not married
- in a stepfamily.

Some reasons for these changes are set out below.

Marriage More people decide to delay marriage or not to marry at all. People who marry later tend to have smaller families.

Contraception Contraception is better today than in the past. It gives women greater control over when and whether they have children.

Employment Changes at work and in the home have helped women to gain more independence. This means that they may be less willing to stay in an unhappy relationship.

Women who want a career tend to have fewer children.

Tolerance Changing attitudes to homosexuality have seen more families led by gay couples and single gay people.

Divorce Separation and divorce have become more common. People often marry again, making step families more common.

Back to basics

Some people are sorry that families have changed. They think that the best thing for society is a child living with two parents who are married to one another.

During the early 1990s the Conservative Prime Minister, John Major, called for a 'back-to-basics' campaign in all areas of life, especially the family. In the late 1990s, both the Conservative and Labour governments suggested new laws to encourage couples seeking a divorce to get help to improve the chances of their staying together.

The laws did not come into force. But governments continue to encourage 'family values'.

ONE-THIRD OF MARRIAGES NOW END I DIVORCE!

? questions

2. Pick the reason you think is the most important reason for the changing family and say why.

3. You are being interviewed for a magazine about your views on these things:
   - living together before marriage
   - living together and having children
   - getting married
   - deciding to stay single
   - living in a large extended family.

   What would you say in reply?

Families

The second part of this unit looks at the questions of abuse and violence in the family.

Abuse and violence

■ Hidden crime

In 2000, the National Society for the Prevention of Cruelty to Children (NSPCC) asked nearly 3,000 young adults about their experiences of childhood. More than nine out of ten reported that their family life as a child had been a warm and happy time.

A few, however, had suffered abuse and neglect. This included:

- being hit or burnt by a parent or carer
- threats
- humiliation
- violence between parents
- neglect
- sexual abuse.

ChildLine

0800 1111

kidscape

NSPCC
Cruelty to children must stop. FULL STOP.™

www.childline.org.uk   020 7730 3300   www.nspcc.org.uk

? question

1. Design a leaflet to persuade people who know a child is being abused or neglected to do something about it. Make sure you explain in your poster:
   - what the abuse or neglect is
   - where help can be found
   (*abuse* – violence, sexual)
   (*neglect* – not fed, clothed, looked after)

■ Smacking children: who's right?

A survey by the Government in 2000 showed that nine out of ten people in England and Wales were in favour of the right of parents to smack their children. However, a year earlier, another study found that 73 per cent favoured a ban, as long as parents were not prosecuted for minor smacks.

'If a parent cannot slipper a child, the world is going potty.'
Judge Ian McLean

'This Labour government believes in parental discipline. Smacking has a part in that. Our law will do nothing to outlaw smacking.'

Paul Boateng MP, when he was Minister for Health

'Smacking children is morally wrong. If people are smacked a lot it's bound to cause problems. But I don't think it should be a punishable offence. That would be an invasion of individual rights.'
Si Piwko, parent

'The NSPCC, along with many children's organisations, is campaigning to make sure that children have the same protection from assaults as adults do. We believe that people should be educated about other options to discipline children.'
Chris Cloke, Head of Child Protection Awareness

'There's a big difference between smacking, hitting and beating. There's no harm in a little slap given at the right time for the right reason.'
Dannii Fortune, parent

2. Summarise both sides of the argument: 'Should parents be allowed to smack children?'
   - give your view and why
   - say what might happen to the law on smacking in the future.

3. How can we reduce family violence? Here are three suggestions:
   - give families more help
   - educate young people and adults about the problem
   - set up a register of people who have committed abuse.

   Give the advantages and disadvantages of one of these ideas.

4. Many victims of domestic crime do not tell anyone about their suffering. What are the possible effects of keeping quiet in this way?

■ United Kingdom

England
As the law stands today, parents, babysitters and child minders do not have the right to hit a child in their care. This is a very recent development.

Wales and Northern Ireland
Consultations are under way to decide whether a change in the law is desirable.

Scotland

A new law is proposed to prevent anyone hitting a child under the age of three.

■ Domestic violence

Research in 1999 revealed that 30 murders occur each year in London because of domestic violence. The study also showed that:

- one woman in four experiences domestic violence
- domestic violence is reported to police in London every 12 minutes.

■ The law

Hitting someone or threatening to do so is a criminal offence. A court can order:

- one partner to stop assaulting or threatening the other
- a person to leave the home.

If the violent partner breaks the court order (called an 'injunction'), they can be sent to prison.

If a victim of domestic violence leaves home to seek help, the council must provide temporary accommodation if the victim is in danger or homeless.

Education

This unit looks at the questions of rights and responsibilities in education. The first part asks, 'How important is a person's right to education?'

Bullies

■ Michelle's story

Michelle is in Year 11. She has no real interest in school. She feels that she achieves very little when she does go.

Michelle was bullied in Years 8 and 9. She told her mum, who told the school. Four girls were responsible. They were seen by the head, Mrs Rogers. The problem finally seemed to go away. During this time, Michelle had got into the habit of not going to school. This continued and her attendance remains poor.

? questions

1. You are Michelle's head of year and you have a meeting with her and her mum to try to get Michelle into school. Come up with a plan to encourage Michelle's attendance.

2. Bullying is a problem in all schools. Complete a charter for children or teachers about what can be done to tackle the problem. Use the headings, 'What you can do if you are bullied' and 'What teachers should do about bullying'.

■ The head's problem

The bullies used to call Michelle names and tip out her bag and go through all her belongings. They made her feel very stupid.

When Mrs Rogers spoke to them, she told them they were damaging Michelle's education. She told the girls they would be excluded if it continued.

? question

3. Should children be permanently excluded for bullying others? Give reasons for your answer.

■ Exclusion headache

Too easy? In 1997 there were nearly 13,000 exclusions a year.

Many of these students were not being educated elsewhere. Some would hang around the streets during school hours committing crime.

In response to this, the Government decided to make it harder for schools to exclude pupils. By the end of 2001, exclusions had fallen to just over 8,000 a year.

School: 49% 53% 52% 61% — 1998 1999 2000 2001

LEA: 42% 43% 44% 46% — 1998 1999 2000 2001

England: 46% 48% 49% 50% — 1998 1999 2000

Too hard? Some heads complained that they were unable to exclude some pupils who deserved it. Immediate exclusion was allowed only on grounds of:

Simranjit

> It's not GOOD that bullies are allowed back into school. They could just pick ANOTHER victim.

- sexual misconduct
- drug dealing
- serious violence (actual or threatened).

In 2002 schools were also allowed to exclude pupils on the spot for carrying weapons or 'serious' bullying.

Marlene

> If they are gone forever it might not be that good because they will carry on OUTSIDE of school. You can punish them and they will know not to do it again. At least in school there are TEACHERS around to stop it.

? question

4. Complete these sentences:
   - An example of bullying that deserves immediate exclusion is ... because ...
   - I agree/disagree that the government should lay down strict rules for excluding pupils because ...

■ Opinion

? question

On this page are the views of some students.

5. Select the view you agree with most and say why.

■ Fair treatment?

If a head teacher excludes a pupil for more than five days in a term, the governors have to decide whether to support the exclusion. The views of parents must be listened to.

In more serious cases excluded pupils can give their side of the story. Parents have the right to appeal against the governors' ruling to an appeal panel set up by the local authority.

Minak

> Expelling BULLIES will help everyone, not just the one who was being bullied, by helping us CARRY ON with our education.

✳ coursework idea

Prepare an assembly to raise awareness of bullying or begin a peer mentoring scheme. Write under the following headings:
- Activity
- Planning and organisation
- Context (facts about bullying)
- Impact (on you and other people)
- Evaluation (how you felt it went)

Education

The right to education

▪ Malcolm

Malcolm is African–Caribbean British. He lives on a large housing estate in a run-down part of London, where many people are unemployed.

Malcolm did well at primary school. But when he went to secondary school he started to get into trouble.

He could not settle down to his GCSEs and was excluded several times. (These are called **fixed-term exclusions**.)

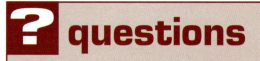

? questions

1. Can you suggest reasons why Malcolm was excluded from school?

2. How may Malcolm be affected if he leaves school without any exam passes?

▪ Excluded from school and society

In 1997 a special unit was set up to look at 'social exclusion'.

Social exclusion happens when people don't get a fair share of the benefits that society has to offer.

They are probably on low income. This means that they are:

- more likely to suffer ill health
- more likely to be the victims of crime
- less likely to do well at school.

If Malcolm fails to get any qualifications, he could end up in this situation.

▪ An educated workforce

In order to compete with other countries, Britain needs a workforce that is skilled and well educated.

Lifelong learning

Years ago it was harder for people who did not succeed at school to have another opportunity to get a good education. Today, the Government encourages people to think of learning as something that happens throughout life.

Alice has just passed her seventh GCSE – at the age of 81. She felt that in the past she had never really had the chance to take any exams. Each year she takes a new course.

David is 21 and is in his second year at university, taking a degree in German and Russian. He works part-time in a restaurant to help pay for his course.

Mehmet comes from Cyprus. He has been living in Britain for more than 30 years. He lost his job and decided to go to college to train as an engineer. Mehmet is now a control room manager in a modern power station.

Paula left school without any GCSEs. She helped at her daughter's playgroup, and decided that she wanted to be trained properly. She became an organiser for the Playgroups Association. She is now taking a degree in child development.

? questions

3. What are the benefits or gains from the extra education that each of these people have had?

4. How important is education to you?

5. Imagine the government had an extra £10 million to spend. What do you think it should be spent on? Which is most important from the list below? Explain why.

education   hospitals
armed forces   transport.
social services

◆ keyword

Fixed-term exclusion
Exclusion from school for a set length of time, which may not be for more than 45 days in a school year.

Education

The final part of this unit asks how students should take part in the running of their schools.

Student voice

No council here

Bernard Jones is the headmaster of a comprehensive school in Oxford. He is liked by the pupils and respected by the staff.

Mr Jones always listens to students before changing anything in his school. He knows every student by name. He says, 'Pupils can always come to me and tell me what's on their minds.'

Surprisingly, Mr Jones is against school councils. He thinks they often don't work. They give the wrong idea about democracy. This is because there are limits to the powers of school councils. Instead he sees all students personally once a year, when they can say whether they want things changed.

Student councils

Recent research has found that about half of all secondary schools in England and Wales have school councils.

Stile Way School has 1,900 students. The school has six houses. Each has a student council. Each house council sends one student to the main school council. This includes the head, teaching and non-teaching staff, a parent and a governor.

Recent issues for discussion:

- new lunchtime and after-school clubs

- whether to have a vending machine with Pot Noodles

- improving the school toilets

- what to do with the £400 they have been given to spend on the school.

? questions

1. What is a school council? Use these words and phrases to help you:
   - group
   - decision making
   - involvement
   - power

2. Is Mr Jones right? Use these words and phrases to help you to give arguments for and against school councils:

For	Against
• participation • democracy • pupil power • working as a group • raising issues	• no real power • pretence • unnecessary

Organisation In most schools one representative from each form is elected to the school council. In large schools this can be up to 50 students. Some schools feel this is too many. They have class groups reporting to a smaller full council.

Havenden Community College has 2,000 students. Every form elects a representative to the school council. This has more than 60 students. Two teachers also attend.

Recent questions for discussion:

• recent changes to the school day

• how students can help in choosing senior staff

• having a school representative on the town's youth council

• where the new Year 10 base should be placed.

? questions

3. Name one similarity and one difference in the organisation of the councils at Stile Way School and Havenden Community College.

4. What important difference do you notice about the questions for discussion in the two councils?

5. One student said, 'We can complain until we're blue in the face about our limited choice of options or the lack of good sex education and drugs education, but we're not really taken seriously unless we're talking about things like locks on the toilet doors and toilet rolls.'

   Complete these sentences:
   • The student is critical of the school council because . . .
   • The situation could be improved by . . .
   • This is likely/unlikely to happen because . . .

6. Do you have a student council at your school? If so, how is it run?

■ Is there a right to be heard?

Britain has signed the United Nations Convention on the Rights of the Child. Article 12 of this sets out the right of 'the child who is capable of forming his/her own views to express those views freely in all matters affecting the child'.

? questions

7. Should all schools be required to have a school council?

8. Are there any issues that should never be discussed by a school council? If so, what are they and why?

Managing the economy

This unit explains some of the decisions governments have to take when running the economy.

Moving target

Most governments would probably like their country to have:

- plenty of jobs for people to do
- stable prices
- enough money for hospitals and schools.

This is not easy, because the economy of a country is always changing.

■ The business cycle

'Boom', 'recession' and 'recovery' are words used to describe the economy of the country at different times.

Boom During a boom things go well and people have more money to spend. Businesses:

- have full order books
- spend money on new equipment
- employ more people.

Recession This brings problems such as these:

- costs rise and push up prices
- people decide not to buy the goods and services on offer
- people are laid off
- some firms close down.

Recovery This happens when:

- business confidence returns
- new jobs are created.

Control

Governments today try to avoid rising prices (called inflation) and unemployment. They do this through:

- taxation – reduces the amount people spend, but money is there for public services
- government spending – creates more jobs and gives people spending power.

■ Taxation

Taxes are money people pay to the government. There are different types of tax:

- *Direct tax:* Taxes on incomes and savings and for businesses on profits.
- *Indirect tax:* Taxes on spending: for example, VAT (value-added tax). This is currently 17.5 per cent on almost all goods and services we buy.

? question

1. Some people believe that we should pay less tax, others say we should pay more. What is your view on this? Here are some opinions to help you:
   - 'What is the point in working hard if you have to pay more tax?'
   - 'If we paid more taxes we would have better hospitals and schools.'
   - 'People should be allowed to keep the money they earn.'

Social security: benefits
£104,000 million

Education: school, colleges, universities
£21,000 million

Health: hospitals, doctors, medical services
£52,000 million

Defence: the armed forces
£24,000 million

International aid: helping poorer countries
£3,000 million

Law and order: police and prisons
£9,000 million

Government spending The Government has to decide how much of the money it raises in taxes will be spent on services.

Spending money on roads, schools and hospitals creates more jobs and puts money back into the economy.

■ Choices

The Chancellor of the Exchequer (the government minister in charge of finance) has to decide how much money will be raised by taxes and how much can then be spent on public services.

Big spenders? In 2002 about £350,000 million was set aside to pay for public services and other kinds of government spending. The pie chart shows where some of this money was spent.

■ Provision of services

Services are provided by other people, not just the Government. For example, sometimes people are cared for in a hospice run by a charity.

This is partly financed by the Health Service, but money also comes from donations from people and organisations who raise money.

Volunteers also work alongside doctors and nurses from the Health Service. An organisation called the League of Friends provides visitors for those who have few relatives.

? questions

2. Put the heading 'Government spending'. Look at the pie chart and write a list in order of the amount that was spent, starting with the greatest.

3. Which of the proposals below would you choose as a spending priority? Give reasons.
   - the police
   - armed forces
   - building motorway
   - hospitals
   - housing
   - social security benefits
   - railways
   - helping poorer people overseas.

Governing ourselves

This unit looks at some of the recent changes in the way that we are governed.

A United Kingdom?

SCOTLAND

N. IRELAND

ENGLAND

WALES

Differences and similarities

Today the United Kingdom has three separate court and legal systems.

England and Wales have one; Scotland and Northern Ireland each have another.
The main lawmaking body in the United Kingdom, however, is Parliament, based in London.

■ Devolution

This means passing power from central to regional government.
In the United Kingdom there is now devolved government in Northern Ireland, Scotland and Wales.

The United Kingdom is made up of England, Northern Ireland, Scotland and Wales. It hasn't always been like this. At one stage the countries were quite separate. Then in:

- 1536 Wales came under English control
- 1707 Union with Scotland
- 1800 the English took control of Ireland
- 1922 independence for southern Ireland, which became known as the Republic of Ireland.

The new Northern Ireland Assembly

In 1998 the new Northern Ireland Assembly was set up.

The National Assembly for Wales

In 1999 a National Assembly for Wales was set up. This followed a referendum in 1997, which asked Welsh voters whether they wanted devolution.

The Scottish Parliament
In 1997, the people in Scotland gave a clear 'yes' to the creation of their own Parliament. This was opened in Edinburgh in 1999.

The National Assembly for Wales, Cardiff

The city mayor

The attack on the Twin Towers in New York on 11 September 2001 brought Rudolph Giuliani to the attention of the world. New Yorkers knew him well.

He had been their city mayor for eight years. He had a reputation for getting things done. He turned New York from the murder capital of the world to one of the safest cities in America.

Under his direction there was a 62 per cent drop in crime – the steepest fall for 30 years.

Good for all? The Government is strongly encouraging cities in Britain to elect their own mayors, with increased powers to manage their area. Those in favour of the idea see it as a way of getting more people interested in local politics. Putting one person in charge makes it much harder for excuses to be offered when things go wrong.

Not everyone agrees. People in Birmingham were against this idea. 'Putting one person in charge of a £2 million budget would be a disaster,' said one councillor. 'Would they really be interested in emptying bins and filling holes in the road?'

? questions

1. Suggest one advantage in people in Wales, Scotland and Northern Ireland having their own government.

2. Can you see any disadvantages with this?

3. Some people now say that England should also have its own Assembly. Others argue for each region – for example, Devon, Cornwall or Yorkshire – having its own Assembly.
   Which of these would you support:
   • give England its own government?
   • give each region its own government?
   • leave things as they are?

4. Give the arguments for and against having a city mayor.

The power of the media

This unit looks at the influence of the media on our lives. It asks whether there should be any changes in the way they work.

The front page

Almost every newspaper puts its main story on the front page. It is where most readers look first. It can influence whether people choose to buy the newspaper.

A sample of recent news headlines.

The senior journalists, including the editor, decide which of the big stories a newspaper will use, and where they will go.

Jonny Wilkinson receives MBE England World Cup Rugby hero Johny Wilkinson has received his MBE at Buckingham Palace.

Migrants influx fear exaggerated The European Parliament's president has said that fear of an influx of people from new EU states is exaggerated.

FORCES OF DARKNESS Retro rockers blitz with three awards.

Violent crime up by 14% Violent crime in England and Wales has risen 14%. Home office figures show.

Wanted . . . Weapons of Mass Destruction CIA offer internet reward for Iraq missiles.

Race attack figures released The latest figures on racist attacks in Northern Ireland show that there were 189 offences committed over the year.

Is Labour right to downgrade cannabis? Is it a dangerous drug that causes addiction or just a harmless herb?

Henry VIII The First King of Football Historians have endence that this notorious king probably enjoyed a kickabout.

? questions

1. You have to decide which three stories opposite you would put on your front page. Give the newspaper a title and space the stories on the page you choose. Write a little bit about the story you pick.

2. Your editor (boss) wants to know why you picked these stories and not the others. What do you say?
   - I picked the three on the front page because . . .
   - I didn't pick the other stories because . . .

In the know

Most of us learn what is happening through the media – newspapers, radio, television, and the Internet.

This places people who own or work for the media in a powerful position. It gives them a huge influence on how we think about world events.

MAIN SOURCE OF WORLD NEWS
Source: Public View 2001

- Newspapers 16%
- Radio 14%
- Television 66%

Readership, by proportion of adult population
Source: Social Trends 2002

Newspaper	Percentage
The Sun	20%
Daily Mirror	12%
Daily Mail	12%
Daily Express	4%
Daily Star	3%
Telegraph	5%
TIMES	3%
Guardian	3%
Independent	1%
FINANCIAL TIMES	1%

Television Television is the main source of news for most people in Britain. However, newspapers are more important for local news.

Newspapers More than half the adult population read a newspaper every day.

? question

3. Research and prepare a report for someone who has no idea of how the newspaper business works in Britain. In your report, include the following:

- A title: 'A report on newspapers in Britain today by …'

- Paragraph 1 – Popularity
- The most popular newspaper is …
    Followed by …
- The least popular newspapers are …

- Paragraph 2 – Purpose
- The purpose of newspapers is to …

- Paragraph 3 – Ownership
- Most newspapers in Britain are owned by four companies …
- The advantage of this is …
- The disadvantage of this is …

■ Ownership and control

Television The BBC began broadcasting radio programmes in 1922. Television started in 1936. BBC programmes are paid for by the TV licence.

Independent Television (ITV) came into existence in 1955.

Channels 3, 4 and 5 are paid for through advertising. Cable and satellite services are paid for by people who pay extra.

Newspapers Newspapers have to make money to survive. Most of the national newspapers in Britain (87 per cent of sales) are produced by four companies. The largest, News International, owns the *Sun*, *The Times*, the *Sunday Times* and the *News of the World*.

The power of the media

Managing the news

Somewhere in Britain

During the Second World War many towns and cities in Britain were heavily bombed. Certain details were kept from the public for fear of giving information to the enemy and lowering morale. Keeping back or controlling information is called censorship.

How far do you go?

After the 11 September attacks on New York and Washington, the British and American governments asked the media in both countries to limit broadcasts of Osama Bin Laden, who praised the attacks and warned that more would follow.

The US government said that broadcasting statements from the man held responsible for the deaths of 2,792 people was not in the interests of the United States.

It could encourage people to fight for him and could contain hidden codes ordering further attacks on the West.

Some people said that this was a mistake. They believed that if Osama Bin Laden wanted to communicate with followers he could still do it – such as through the Internet or by mobile phone.

They also said that the real reason for this censorship was both governments' fear that it could reduce support for the war against them.

Bomb damage after an air raid on London, 1940. Photographs like this were not published until the war had ended.

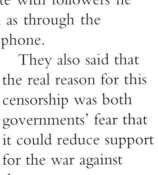

? question

1. The difficulties of deciding whether or not to censor broadcasts was discussed at great length on the Internet. Here are three extracts from messages published on the BBC website.

> **>Phil H, UK**
>
> 'By showing these tapes, the media are acting as pawns in Osama Bin Laden's campaign.'

> **>C.Meyer, US**
>
> 'Not to censor these tapes would be extremely short-sighted and ultimately irresponsible.'

> **>Safarali Senego, India**
>
> 'Let the truth be told. Do not give to the people only the western or eastern version of the truth.'

How do you respond to each of these points? On balance, what action would you recommend?

The role of the media

In 1988 a programme was made called *Death on the Rock*. It investigated the deaths of three members of the IRA (the Irish Republican Army), shot by the SAS (Special Air Service) in Gibraltar.

Since the 1970s, members of the IRA had carried out terrorist attacks in Northern Ireland and on the UK mainland.

The Government were against this programme being broadcast. Margaret Thatcher, Prime Minister at the time, claimed that the programme just gave the terrorists publicity.

More recently, some of the press has been criticised for failing to support fully the war in Afghanistan.

How far do you go?

News reports rarely give the basic facts. What is chosen and the language used influence the reader.

Sometimes managing the news goes further. Mrs Thatcher wanted to draw attention to the need to clear our towns and cities of litter. Papers and cans were deliberately dropped on the grass in a London park. This meant the Prime Minister could be photographed doing something about the problem by picking them up!

? questions

2. A terrorist organisation has carried out many terrorist acts because they want independence from Britain. Complete a debate page for your local paper. The title is 'Should programmes that are favourable to this terrorist organisation be shown on television?'

Yes	No
I think that ____ Because ____	I think that ____ Because ____

3. Produce a front-page headline and a few sentences from a newspaper that is against:
   - spending more on education
     or
   - having the euro currency.

Freedom to publish

This unit discusses whether limits should be placed on stories that appear in the media.

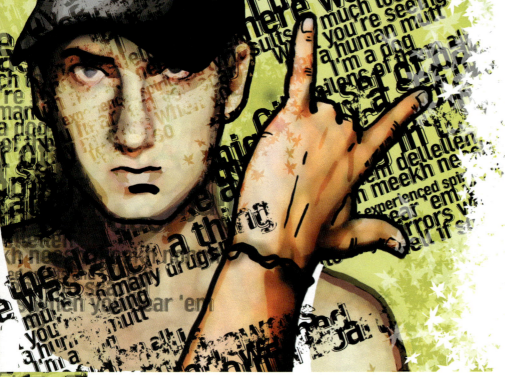

Number one

The violent content of the Eminem's songs and anti-women and anti-gay words have led people to call for his music to be banned.

However, not everyone is offended. 'I don't think people will go out and start beating and killing people because of this album,' said one singer. Others defended Eminem's right to freedom of expression.

? question

1. Do you think music from artists such as Eminem should be banned? Explain your answer?

Violence There is concern about violence in the media because:

- it makes us less sensitive to injury and suffering
- people copy what they see
- people are seen solving problems with

violence rather than by discussion and compromise.

Some research has shown a link between violence in the media and violent behaviour. Other work questions this. It is difficult to make a link because antisocial behaviour is the result of many factors, not just watching media violence.

Sex Until the 1960s in American films 'excessive and lustful kissing' was forbidden. When a man and woman were pictured on a couch, each was required to have one foot on the floor.

Film and television today would be very different if this were still the case. A survey carried out in 1999 found that people were becoming more tolerant of sex on television. However, sex in some soaps was thought by many to be unacceptable. Women and older people were more likely to be against sex on TV.

? question

2. Some people blame television for poor behaviour. They feel that sex and violence on TV encourage us to copy them.

Draw a line on your page and copy the boxes. Then put a mark on this line where you think your viewpoint lies, and say why you feel this:

| Watching sex and violence definitely has an influence | Watching sex and violence doesn't have an influence |

■ Private lives

The radio presenter Sara Cox did not expect that pictures of her and her husband naked by the pool at their holiday villa would be shown in a Sunday newspaper. A photographer had rented the house next door to where the couple were staying, so that he could take the pictures.

Sara Cox claimed that this was an unreasonable invasion of her privacy.

Privacy Anyone who believes that their privacy has been invaded by the press can:

- take their complaint to the Press Complaints Commission, who can order the newspaper to publish an apology
- take the case to court to stop publication or to seek damages, but this is expensive
- use the *Human Rights Act*, saying that they have a right to a private life.

To win a case with the Press Complaints Commission, they have to prove that the information was 'not in the public interest'.

Balance It is difficult to balance press freedom and respect for privacy. Newspapers and television news have to report important information. But they should not unreasonably invade people's privacy.

? question

- The ex-boyfriend of a *Coronation Street* star sells his story to a newspaper. This includes details of their sex life.
- In his year between school and university, Prince William is photographed hiking and crossing a river in Chile. The pictures are published in a British magazine.
- A television personality visits a prostitute, who sells the story to a newspaper. The man tries to stop the story being published.

3. Copy the table below and put each of the above cases under one of the headings. Explain your choices.

Acceptable	Unacceptable

Left: Until he was 18, the press agreed not to publish pictures of Prince William without the permission of the Royal Family.

Voting and elections

This unit looks at the different ways in which people can vote. It asks whether parts of our voting system should be changed.

A problem for the council

Labour councillors in Bristol had a problem. The cost of providing **public services** in the city was going up and up. The biggest expense was education.

To continue to give the people of Bristol the education services they were used to meant finding more money. The only way to do this was to increase the **council tax**.

The Labour council had only two more councillors than the Liberal Democrats.

Local elections were coming up in May. Labour could lose control of the council.

A decision had to be taken about spending more on public services – and it had to be taken quickly.

? question

1. Role-play a conversation between two Labour councillors discussing their problem for Bristol Council.

■ What the council did

- They held a referendum (a vote on a single issue). People voted on whether to increase council tax or keep it the same.
- Voters were warned that having no tax rise would probably mean cuts in the education service.

■ The result

- Out of the 278,000 electors in Bristol, 40 per cent voted in the referendum.
- Of these, 54 per cent voted against an increase in council tax.

■ Reaction

- Teachers were angry. They threatened to go on strike if any teacher lost their job.
- The teachers said that one in five secondary students in Bristol went to a private school.
- They also said that some people in Bristol sent their children to schools in other authorities' areas.

? question

2. What do you think about the decision to have a referendum? Explain your answer.

I DISAGREE! IT'S MY RIGHT!

Democracy

■ What does it mean?

The decision on whether to increase council tax in Bristol was taken through a process of democracy.

There are two types of democracy:

Direct democracy When people make their decisions together as a single group.

Representative democracy When people elect representatives to take decisions on their behalf, e.g. a local councillor, an MP or a school councillor.

Representative democracy also:

- responds to public opinion
- has regular and free elections
- allows people to criticise what it does
- protects the rights of individuals and minority groups.

■ Referendum

A referendum is when people are asked to vote on a political issue.

In 1975 there was a referendum asking if people agreed with Britain's membership of the European Community. In 1998, the people of Wales had a referendum on whether they wanted a separate assembly.

Some would like to have more referendums. They feel that they give people more of a say in decisions that affect them. Others disagree, believing that some issues are too complex to be reduced to one or two simple questions.

? questions

3. Divide your page into two with the headings 'Direct democracy' and 'Representative democracy'.

   Put the following issues under the heading you think would be better suited. Say why you have put it there.
   - whether to adopt the euro as our currency
   - whether the country should go to war
   - whether we should have more religious or faith schools
   - whether to ban smoking in all public places.

4. Which type of democracy do you think is better? Why?

5. What issue(s) would you have a referendum on and why?

❖ keywords

Council tax
A tax paid to the council by most householders based on the value of their property.

Local elections
Elections to choose councillors for the local council.

Public services
Services needed by the community as a whole, e.g. street lighting, education, waste disposal.

Voting and elections

The right to vote

The present voting age of 18 was set in 1969.

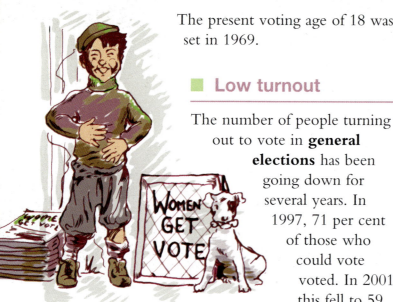

■ Low turnout

The number of people turning out to vote in **general elections** has been going down for several years. In 1997, 71 per cent of those who could vote voted. In 2001, this fell to 59 per cent.

Natalie's story 'I did not vote in the last election. Do you want to know why?

'Imagine this. There are two blokes who fancy me. I don't fancy them. If I was forced, I suppose I would say that one of them is not quite as bad as the other. But my heart's not in it. So I decide to ignore them both and wait for someone better.

'That's why I didn't vote in the last election. It wasn't because I had better things to do, or it was raining or because I couldn't be bothered. It was because there wasn't any party that believed in what I believed in.'

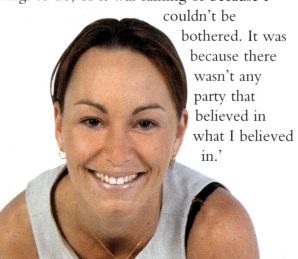

? question

1. Natalie has told you her reasons for not voting. How would you reply to her?

   Some arguments for voting are given below:

   No respect Not protecting our rights shows no respect for those who fought and died in two world wars.

   No control You are letting politicians do what they like.

   No say You are throwing away the chance to have a say in the way the country is run.

   Responsibility You have a responsibility to vote as a citizen.

   Sets a bad example Where would this country be if nobody voted at all?

   Struggle You should remember the struggle that women had to get the right to vote.

■ Reasons

In 2001 the largest drop in voting was among those in the 18–24 age range, with 20 per cent fewer voting than in 1997. Here are some reasons:

Contentment People were happy with the way things were.

All the same There was little difference between one political party and another.

Foregone conclusion The Labour Party would win the election (which it did), therefore no point in voting.

Irrelevant People felt that politics didn't affect them.

What can be done?

Here are some suggestions to increase the numbers who turn out to vote.

Easy vote Let people vote from home by phone or the Internet – or in their local supermarket.

Education Teach more about politics at school.

Incentives Allow people who vote to pay less in tax, or make voting compulsory, as in Australia.

Presentation The political parties should do more to interest voters.

Real people Make politicians seem more like ordinary people. Increase the number of female, black and Asian candidates.

Lower the voting age to 16

For: If young people can get married at 16 and work and pay taxes, they are old enough to vote.

Against: Young people wouldn't understand enough about politics to use their vote wisely.

? questions

2. Your local MP asks why people didn't vote in 2001. Explain to him or her the reasons for this.

3. How do you think turnout at elections could be increased? Use the information in the book and your own ideas to prepare a speech titled: 'How to increase turnout at elections: a strategy'.

❖ keyword

General election
An election to choose the MPs who will form a new Parliament, held every five years or less.

Election to Parliament

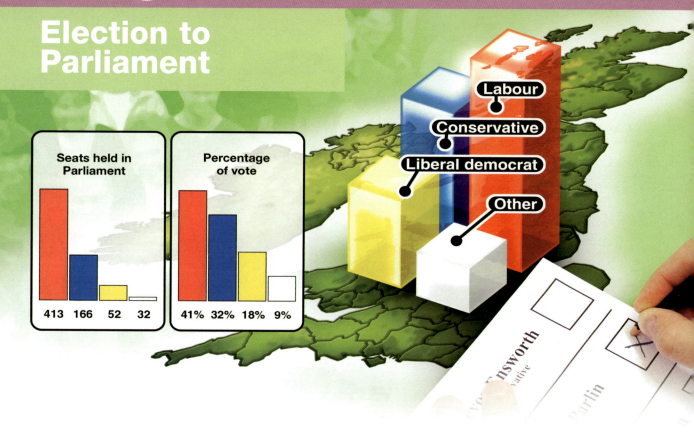

Seats held in Parliament

413 166 52 32

Percentage of vote

41% 32% 18% 9%

Labour
Conservative
Liberal democrat
Other

Constituencies

There are 659 MPs in Parliament for the whole of the United Kingdom.

Almost all MPs represent a political party. The local area they represent is called a constituency.

Elections

If an MP dies or resigns, a by-election is called to elect a new MP for their constituency.

At least every five years a general election must take place. Voters have the chance to re-elect or change their MP.

The party with the greatest number of MPs forms the government. The party leader becomes Prime Minister.

Voting

First-past-the-post Votes for general and by-elections are counted on a 'first-past-the-post' system. People each cast one vote and the winning candidate is the one with the most votes.

? questions

Above are the results of the United Kingdom general election, 2001.

1. Which party won the election in 2001?

2. If seats in Parliament had been given according to the percentage of the votes, how would Parliament be different?

Other voting systems

In recent years people have voted for the:

- European Parliament
- National Assembly for Wales
- Scottish Parliament
- London Assembly
- Northern Ireland Assembly.

CANDIDATE	PARTY	Y... O... C...
EVANS, Annabel	Labour	
FERGUSON, Robert	Conservative	
KINGSLEY, Mica	Liberal Democrat	
JONES, Martin	Plaid Cymru	
RAMIREZ, Joseph	Green Party	
SAMPSON, Emma	Independent Soci...	

In a constituency where four seats are available, the four candidates who come top become the MPs. This system shows which party is really popular.

None of these has used the first-past-the-post system. Instead, other systems have been used. These are listed below.

List system In the election for the European Parliament in 1999, voters cast one vote – not for a person, but for a party. Each party got the number of seats equal to the share of its vote. If a party won 20 per cent of the vote, it got 20 per cent of the seats.

Additional-member system Everyone has two votes. The first is for the person you want to represent your constituency. This is the one who gets the most votes.

The second is for your favourite *party*. Further seats are given so they are in line with the votes cast. This system has been used in the elections for:

- the Assemblies for Wales and London
- the Scottish Parliament.

Single transferable vote The seats in the constituency are listed. So are the names of all those standing for election. The voter has to number the candidates in order of preference.

The counting is difficult because it uses people's second, third and fourth choices to decide who is the most popular candidate.

? questions

3. Have a group election using first-past-the-post and the single transferable vote systems.
   - **Step 1:** Select a number of candidates from the class. Choose at least one for each of the three main parties. You could include smaller parties, such as the Green Party.
   - **Step 2:** Make sure everyone has a list of the candidates, an outline of their policies and a ballot paper.
   - **Step 3:** Everyone puts a 1 against the candidate of their first choice, and a 2 against the candidate of their second choice.
   - **Step 4:** Collect in the ballot papers and count the first-choice votes. This produces the winning candidate (and party) by first-past-the-post.
   - **Step 5:** Add the second-choice votes to the first-choice ones. Work out the total number of votes for each candidate. This uses the system of the single transferable vote.

4. Compare your results using the two systems. What do you notice?

Party politics

This unit looks at political parties. It asks what influence the media have on our political views.

Join the party

■ Imagine

When Channel 4 carried out a poll to find the all-time top 100 British Number 1 singles, first place went to John Lennon's 'Imagine'.

Many people probably wouldn't want to live like this – 'imagine no possessions' – but, for some, the words of the song do say at least something about the kind of society that they would like to see.

Imagine no possessions,
I wonder if you can,
No need for greed or hunger,
A brotherhood of man,
Imagine all the people
Sharing all the world...

? question

1. Say four things you would change to make life better:
   - at school
   - in the local area
   - in the country
   - in the world.

■ Ideas into action

Protest Sometimes we are so concerned about a problem that we take action ourselves. When a local school is threatened with closure, parents, children and teachers may protest either as individuals or as a group.

Pressure groups If the issue is of wider importance we might join or support a national or international group. The RSPCA and Oxfam are examples of these. Organisations of this kind are called pressure groups.

Political parties Political parties are organisations interested in a much wider range of issues than pressure groups. They also tend to have certain principles or ideas.

The Conservative Party
- has stood for the right of people to make the most of their talents
- is against government interference
- supports the Queen
- sees Britain playing an important and independent role in the world.

The Labour Party
- has always tried to improve the situation of working people, for example through council housing and the National Health Service, which it introduced in 1945.

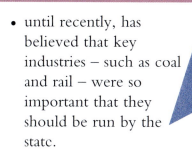

- until recently, has believed that key industries – such as coal and rail – were so important that they should be run by the state.

The Liberal Democrat Party
- seeks to protect individual rights and freedoms
- supports close links with the remainder of Europe
- wants higher taxes to pay for public services such as education
- wants a change in the voting system, which it sees as unfair.

Other parties in England and Wales include:
- Plaid Cymru, which aims to get independence for Wales
- the Green Party, which wants to produce a fairer society with less damage to the environment.

▮ Tolerance?

The British National Party (BNP) puts out misleading information and ideas, particularly about immigrants and refugees. It is very critical of black and white people mixing and says that the presence of immigrants and refugees is linked to problems in healthcare, education and housing. The BNP wants immigrants to go back to their original homes.

▮ The law

Freedom of expression is allowed under the *Human Rights Act* but this may be limited to preserve public order and protect the rights of others. It is an offence to publish and to possess racist material.

British National Party supporters

? questions

2. Split into groups of six. Each person should tell the others at least one thing about their party. The parties you will be are:
   - Conservative
   - Labour
   - Liberal Democrat
   - Plaid Cymru
   - Green Party
   - BNP

3. Should the BNP be allowed to state their views?

4. Explain what a political party and a pressure group are.

Party politics

Newspapers

Read all about it

Below is the *Sun*'s front page of 6 October 1998. The former Conservative leader William Hague's head is attached to the body of a parrot pictured hanging upside down. The newspaper went on to say, 'Like Monty Python's parrot, it has fallen off its perch.'

How do articles like this affect the way in which people vote?

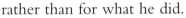

THIS PARTY IS NO MORE... IT HAS CEASED TO BE... THIS IS A DEAD PARTY.

Newspapers and political parties

Most national newspapers tend to favour one political party in particular – although this isn't as fixed it used to be.

Until the mid-1990s the *Daily Mirror*, the *Guardian* and the *Independent* were the only national daily papers not to support the Conservatives. But, by the time of the 2001 general election, most newspapers were recommending that their readers vote Labour. Only the *Daily Mail* and *Daily Telegraph* remained Conservative.

Bias

Newspapers have political influence through how and what they report.

Michael Foot, who led the Labour Party in the 1980s, is remembered by many people for what he wore, rather than for what he did.

At a Remembrance Day service in London he was photographed wearing an old jacket. Some thought this was not suitable for such an occasion. Newspapers that didn't like Labour gave this picture a lot of coverage. They suggested that a party whose leader dressed in this way was not fit for government.

Profit All newspapers, and much of television and radio, are businesses trying to make a profit.

? questions

1. Your mum or dad reads the *Daily Mail*, but isn't aware of its politics. Explain to them how newspapers can be politically biased. Begin with:
   - 'All newspapers are politically biased. For example . . .'

2. Tell the story of how Michael Foot's career was harmed by newspapers.

3. Try to find a newspaper article that is trying to influence the political view of the reader – stick it on a large piece of paper and highlight words or phrases that show bias.

Radio and television

Balance

Radio and television are under tighter control than newspapers. Unlike newspapers, radio and TV must not tell their viewers whom to vote for in an election. In fact on voting day they can only say that an election is taking place.

Public opinion

Newspapers, radio and television, and the political parties themselves carry out surveys into which party people favour and how they intend to vote. These are called opinion polls.

Some people feel we should ban opinion polls during the period of an election. They say that opinion polls influence the way people vote. Stating that one party is ahead of another can affect the way people will vote. For example, if people think Labour are going to win they may be less likely to turn out to vote.

SO, GENTLEMEN, ARE YOU FOR OR AGAINST THE *EURO?*

? questions

4. Prepare arguments for and against opinion polls to be given as a speech to your class.

5. In 2002 the BBC asked people in Wales how they would vote in a referendum on the euro. These were the results.
   - 41 per cent said they would vote 'Yes' to joining the common currency
   - 40 per cent said they would vote 'No'
   - 15 per cent replied 'Don't know'
   - 4 per cent said they would not vote at all.

a) How might a newspaper *in favour* of Britain's membership of the euro present these figures?

b) How might they be presented by a newspaper that is *against* our membership of the euro?

c) How would you interpret the figures in an *accurate and balanced* way?

Campaigning

This unit shows how community action can be used to bring about change. It asks what people need to do to improve their chances of success.

Home alone

Florence Okolo arrived in Britain from Nigeria to join her husband. He was a student in Manchester. Florence brought with her their two daughters. A year later, she had a baby boy.

One year later Florence and her husband separated. Florence's husband went back to Nigeria, with his son.

Florence stayed in Manchester. She had a home and a job, and she belonged to the local church. The girls went to primary school. They were all part of the community.

Florence and her family no longer had any legal right to remain in Britain. They did not have British citizenship. Four years after arriving here, Florence got a letter from the **Home Office** ordering her and her daughters to leave.

Florence had to persuade the Home Office that she and her daughters should not be made to leave (deported). This would be difficult to do alone. She had no family in Britain and little money.

? question

1. What do you think Florence could do? Whom could she find to help her with her case?

Help

Florence went to a solicitor. He agreed to help her. He suggested that she should ask for help from her daughters' school.

The school said they would do as much as they could.

? questions

2. You are Florence Okolo as she arrived at the solicitor's office to explain her case. Tell the solicitor your story. Include the following points:
   - arrival in Britain from Nigeria
   - two daughters and a baby boy
   - separation from husband
   - after four years, ordered to leave.

3. Imagine you are the headteacher of the girls' school. Write a list of five things you could do to start the campaign.

■ Tactics

Over the next four years Florence, her solicitor, the school and the church did as much as they could. This is what they did.

- *Putting the case* The solicitor prepared the documents for permission to remain in Britain. When this failed he prepared the papers for an appeal to the Home Secretary.
- *Support* Letters, asking for help, were written to Florence's local MP and the city council in Manchester.
- *Publicity* Florence's supporters wrote letters, made posters and talked to the media.

They organised marches and demonstrations, trying to make sure that the newspapers, radio or television covered them.

They held rallies in Manchester. They had a demonstration in London outside the Houses of Parliament. They involved children from the girls' school.

■ Success

The Home Office at first turned down Florence's application. Then her appeal was rejected. With few chances remaining, her supporters arranged for her to meet the Home Secretary in person. A month after this meeting, Florence received a letter giving her permission to stay in Britain.

? question

4. Florence is interviewed on the radio about her story and the campaign. Think of five questions you would ask her and role-play how you think she would have answered them. You could do this activity in pairs: e.g.:
   - Tell us the background to your case.
   - What did you do first?

◆ keyword

Home Office
A Government department with responsibilities that include law and order and immigration. The Home Secretary is the head of the Home Office.

Campaigning

We want our bus back!

■ Bus stop

The notice in the paper read, 'As from 1 March the 7.55 a.m. service to Bedford will be withdrawn.'

'It's so annoying,' said Lena to her mum. 'We need that to get us to school. If they take it off, we'll have to leave home at five past seven.'

'You could find out why they're doing it,' said her mum, 'and write a letter of complaint.'

? question

1. The next morning Lena asked some of her friends on the bus if they could do anything together to save the service. Here are some of the answers she received:
   - 'It's not our responsibility.'
   - 'No one will listen to us, we're just kids.'
   - 'We won't go to school.'
   - 'It's up to the bus company what it wants to do.'
   - 'We should get teachers or parents to do something about it.'

   Which is the only one of these statements that says that something could be done? Choose one of the other comments and say what you think about it.

■ Starting off

Lena and two of her friends decided to write to complain. In the letter they asked why the 7.55 bus was being withdrawn. They explained how much they needed the service.

The reply said that not enough people used the service. It did not make enough money. The company was sorry but the service would still be changed.

? question

2. Write a letter to the bus company from Lena explaining the problem and what you want to happen.

■ Action

The three friends organised a petition. They collected signatures from everyone who used the bus. They took some photographs of this and sent the pictures to the local newspaper.

They sent the petition to the bus company. They made posters for display in local shops.

They asked the school for help. The head suggested that Lena write to the county council. This has the power to keep important services going. The head and school governors also wrote a letter.

CHILDREN'S PETITION to save bus

'We arranged a meeting with our local county councillor, and wrote to our MP. We also kept the paper informed about our campaign,' said Lena. 'Twice we made it onto the front page.

'We persuaded the county council to talk to the bus company. The council has some money that they can use for a service if they feel it's worthwhile. Finally they reached an agreement. Six weeks after our campaign began, the bus company decided not to cut the 7.55.'

■ Pressure groups

Groups of people campaigning for change are called pressure groups. They can be local and very small, like Lena and her friends; or they can be much larger with international connections. Greenpeace and Amnesty International are examples of these.

? question

5. What is the difference between a pressure group and a political party?

✳ coursework idea

If you belong to a pressure group write about what the group does and what you do towards it, its strengths and weaknesses.

? questions

3. Draw a storyboard showing the action Lena and her friends took. Put the heading 'We want our bus back'. Finish the storyboard by showing the result and why you think it was successful.

4. Find out about any local or school campaign people have been involved in and prepare a speech on this campaign for the class.

Big world, small world

This unit examines some of the benefits and drawbacks of globalisation.

Globalisation

■ Long haul

In 1994 McDonald's sued two protestors, Helen Steel and David Morris, over the contents of a leaflet that they had given out on behalf of London Greenpeace.

The leaflet, headed 'What's wrong with McDonald's?', strongly criticised:

- the food sold by the company
- how the company was run.

McDonald's said the criticisms were unfair. It asked those responsible to take back their comments. Some agreed, but Helen Steel and David Morris did not, and legal action followed.

It took almost three years for both sides to deliver their evidence. McDonald's used a large team of lawyers. Helen Steel and David Morris carried out their own defence. The judge decided that most of the allegations made in the leaflet were untrue. It awarded McDonald's £110,000 damages, later reduced on appeal to £40,000.

■ Worldwide scale

One point made in the leaflet was about how big McDonald's was. The McDonald's Corporation has more than 28,000 restaurants in 120 countries. McDonald's is not alone in

? question

1. Complete a newspaper front page on this story. Think of a headline and a few sentences about this story. Useful words and phrases:
   - leaflet
   - Greenpeace
   - McDonald's
   - court case
   - result.

this. Many companies have bases all over the world.

Companies who have bases in many countries are called 'multinationals'. 'Globalisation' describes the situation in which more and more businesses operate throughout the world – and not just in one or two countries.

The word was used first in the 1980s, but the idea itself goes back more than 500 years.

The long view Between the fifteenth and nineteenth centuries, Britain, and other countries, took over many parts of the world. In doing this, they took their languages and their religions, and set up governments like those at home.

Local people were used as cheap labour and were moved from one area to another against their will. Millions of Africans were shipped to work in the Caribbean and America as slaves.

Britain and other countries made a lot of money from the lands they took over. Spices, coffee and tea appeared in Europe for the first time and were known on a global scale.

■ The situation today

Airline tickets are now sometimes cheaper than rail fares.

Globalisation (when the world seems closer together and linked) has happened for many reasons.

- *Communications* – phones, faxes and computers make it easy to contact people in many parts of the world.

Sending emails by computer is very cheap.

- *Transport* – there is a lot more movement around the world because it is cheaper.

Politics The break-up of the Soviet Union in the 1990s has increased trade with Russia and countries in Eastern Europe.

Size matters There are Asda supermarkets all over Britain. The company started in 1965 but was taken over in 1999 by Wal-Mart, an American company.

In 2001 Wal-Mart had the largest sales of any company in the world. The figures below show how large some businesses have become.

2001 Turnover

Wal-Mart Stores	General Motors	Ford Motor Co.	Philip Morris
$219 billion	$177 billion	$162 billion	$72 billion

2001 GDP

Belgium	Turkey	Denmark	Pakistan
$226 billion	$199 billion	$162 billion	$61 billion

Big world, small world

Anti-globalisation

DEFEND OUR FORESTS
CLEARCUT THE WTO

◼ Protest

In November 1999, 100,000 people marched through the streets of Seattle in the United States of America. Since then protests have also taken place in London, Berlin, Moscow and Prague. These protests have all occurred when world leaders have been meeting to discuss important economic issues.

These people are saying that globalisation causes more harm than good. Some of the protests have been violent, causing damage to buildings and shops. In 2001 in Genoa, a protester was killed as he attacked the police.

People who protest think that world trade helps big business rather than ordinary people.

Targets Large anti-globalisation protests have tended to be held at meetings of the World Trade Organisation, the International Monetary Fund and the World Bank. These are organisations that promote trade and give loans to help countries in crisis.

The protestors believe that the rules governing world trade tend to meet the interests of large business corporations, rather than the needs of ordinary people.

Big businesses take notice only of their **shareholders** and the protests happen because people have no way of showing the World Trade Organisation or the World Bank how they really feel. Other people think the protests are just an excuse for causing trouble and vandalism.

❓ question

1. Complete the following:
   - Globalisation means ...
   - Protesters feel that big businesses ...
   - Asda is owned by Wal-Mart. This company now has the ...
   - Some protesters smash up buildings such as those of McDonald's in important cities. They do this because they feel they have ...

120 **Global citizenship**

The case for globalisation . . .

Examples of globalisation include:

- Japanese companies set up electronics and car factories in Britain
- a joint British and Dutch company makes and sells ice cream in China
- Kenyan farmers send flowers and vegetables to Europe.

How things are better as a result of globalisation:

- living standards for all improve
- there are more jobs, and technology develops
- many companies help local communities
- we have a variety of goods
- we understand people living in other countries better.

. . . and the case against

- a few companies have a lot of power in the world
- environmental concerns are ignored
- foreign investors will pull out if there are better opportunities elsewhere
- imports damage the home industries
- local producers are squeezed out
- the workers have low pay and poor working conditions in overseas companies.

coursework idea

For coursework you could try to find two newspaper articles about globalisation with different views of it.

- explain what the articles say
- put in the background: for example, what is globalisation? Give examples
- say how each view might be biased (one-sided)
- give your own opinion on this issue
- say why other views might be different from yours
- explain the impact of this issue on different groups
- say what might happen in the future.

? questions

2. A worker in a factory making sports equipment in the Far East earns about £50 per month. This is much less than a British worker earns. But £50 is more than the worker would earn if the British company were not there.

   Discuss this situation in groups and come up with a list of points for and against this state of affairs.

3. Explain what globalisation is.

keyword

Shareholder
Someone who invests (buys shares) in a company.

Big world, small world

Trade

The end of the line

After making bicycles for more than a 100 years, the Raleigh factory in Nottingham closed down in 2002 and the business moved to China. Bicycles can be made in China for 25 per cent less than in Britain.

? question

1. Imagine your mother had worked at the Raleigh factory in Nottingham for 25 years and lost her job when the factory moved to China. You are being interviewed by the local newspaper about the effect on your family. What might you say?

Terms and conditions

When a factory is built abroad, it brings work to the area, but wage rates are often lower than they would be in Britain.

Fair game? Some multinational companies make sports and leisure wear. Their factories are in less developed countries. Companies such as Nike and Adidas have been criticised for making their workers work long hours for low pay.

Small steps A 2002 Oxfam study of factories in Indonesia, employing workers to make Nike and Adidas shoes, found that some improvements had been made in recent years. However, its conclusion still makes grim reading.

Power and profit

Nike and Adidas make huge profits. For example, Nike's income for 2001 was £390 million. In 2001 the *Los Angeles Times* reported that the company was paying Tiger Woods £100 million to promote its products.

Oxfam
- *Wages* With full-time wages as low as $US2 (£1.30), workers live in extreme poverty and those with children must either send them to distant villages to be looked after by relatives or else go into debt to meet their basic needs.

Oxfam
- *Working conditions* Workers report that they continue to be shouted at and humiliated and to work in dangerous conditions.

Oxfam
- *Unions* Workers have reason to fear that active union involvement could lead them to be dismissed, jailed or physically assaulted.

■ Fair shares

Almost all manufactured goods go through several stages before they reach the customer. At each one, the worker, the factory owner and the retailer (shop) will need to be paid. But how much should they get?

? questions

2. If a pair of trainers is £80, how much should each of the groups below be given?

Worker	Factory owner	Owner of brand	Retailer

Do you think that this is really what happens to the money? Explain your answer.

■ Taking action

A quarter of the people on this planet live in poverty. There are 1.2 billion people who live on less than 65p per day.

In the mid-1990s, the governments of many countries, including Britain, agreed to try to cut this by half by 2015. This involves:

- giving aid
- training

- helping them to sell their goods
- removing their debt.

In 1972 Britain signed an agreement under which industrial countries would give 0.7 per cent of their wealth in overseas aid. In 2001 the figure was 0.36 per cent.

? question

3. You are organising a fundraising event in school for an overseas charity. Many of your year group refuse to help. They say that charity begins at home. How would you persuade them to take part?

Global warming

This unit asks what action should be taken about changes in world climate.

The problem

Breakaway

The Antarctic ice sheet is the largest body of ice on the planet. It holds 90 per cent of the earth's fresh water.

It is quite normal for small parts of the ice sheet to break off – these form icebergs. They gradually melt as they drift north.

Scientists have known for many years that ice caps over both the North and South Poles are melting. However, in early 2002, two very large pieces of ice broke off the Antarctic ice sheet – about the size of Norfolk. It is believed that this was a very important sign of global warming.

Evidence

Temperatures throughout the world are gradually rising. A big increase has been recorded over the last 25 years. Temperatures in the 1990s were the warmest on record. Scientists noticed a further rise in world temperatures early in 2002.

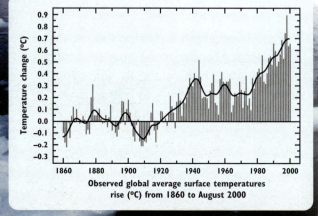

Observed global average surface temperatures rise (°C) from 1860 to August 2000

Explanation

Climate change over long periods of time is quite normal, but scientists agree that the changes since the 1980s are not part of this natural pattern.

The earth is surrounded by a blanket of gas that stops temperatures falling too low. Gases from the gas, coal and oil that we burn have changed the make-up of this blanket. It now holds in more heat than it did in the past, and this causes temperatures on Earth to rise.

- the sun warms the atmosphere
- heat is sent back into space or becomes trapped in a layer of gases around the earth; without this layer, temperatures on earth would be 30 degrees lower
- burning fossil fuels has changed the layer of gas
- heat that would normally escape is trapped.

■ Consequences

- there are more hot days in summer and fewer very cold days
- there are extremes of weather such as high winds, floods and droughts.

? questions

1. Explain what global warming is.

2. Produce a poster that tells people what global warming is and the effects it might have.

■ Predictions

- *Sea levels* The melting of glaciers and ice caps could, by the end of the twenty-first century, cause sea levels to rise. This would put a number of places at risk. Low-lying parts of Bangladesh would be flooded, as would parts of major coastal cities such as London and New York.

- *Farming* Some crops become impossible to grow. This is likely to a) increase food prices, b) give rise to shortages, c) affect some parts of the world worse than others.

- *Flora and fauna* Some species of animals and plants will disappear.

- *Natural disasters* There could be an increase in natural disasters such as flooding, drought, disease and forest fires. All areas would be at risk, but disasters would happen more often in developing countries. They have fewer ways of dealing with them.

The solution

■ Who's who?

There are 210 countries in the world. The tables below show the ten with the highest carbon dioxide emissions, and the ten with the lowest.

The highest …

🇺🇸	USA	1 480 000 000 tons
🇨🇳	China	840 000 000 tons
🇷🇺	Russia	390 000 000 tons
🇯🇵	Japan	300 000 000 tons
🇮🇳	India	280 000 000 tons
🇩🇪	Germany	220 000 000 tons
🇬🇧	United Kingdom	140 000 000 tons
🇨🇦	Canada	120 000 000 tons
🇮🇹	Italy	110 000 000 tons
🇲🇽	Mexico	100 000 000 tons

…and the lowest

	Uganda	20 000 000 tons
	Cambodia	20 000 000 tons
	Zaire	10 000 000 tons
	Afghanistan	10 000 000 tons
	Mali	10 000 000 tons
	Burundi	10 000 000 tons
	Ethiopia	10 000 000 tons
	Chad	less than 10 000 000 tons
	Namibia	less than 10 000 000 tons
	Turks & Caicos Islands	less than 10 000 000 tons

CO2 emissions, 1998. Source: Oak Ridge National Laboratory and the University of North Dakota

■ Warning

The phrase 'greenhouse effect' was first used in 1827. In 1938 a British weather expert found a rise in world temperatures over the previous 50 years.

It was not until the late 1970s that the nations of the world began to discuss global warming in any detail. One of the most important steps was taken at the Earth Summit, held in Rio de Janeiro in Brazil in 1992.

? questions

1. Look at the figures to the left and complete the following.

   The highest emissions are from … because …

   The lowest emissions are from … because …

2. Leaders at the Earth Summit needed to decide how to reduce carbon dioxide emissions worldwide. Here are some of their choices:

   A Let every country decide for itself by how much it should reduce its emissions.

   B Every country should cut its emissions by a fixed percentage, e.g. 10 per cent, before a certain date.

   C The richest industrial countries, such as the United States, Japan, Britain and Germany, should reduce their emission levels before those of poorer, non-industrial countries.

   Which is the best choice and why?

■ Progress

The Rio summit came to some important agreements:

- sustainable development – to meet our present needs without damage to the environment
- each local council to have a local programme of action called **Agenda 21** – this would put sustainable development into action
- to reduce the levels of carbon dioxide with industrial nations first and developing countries later.

Sustainable development This means developing without damaging the environment or using up valuable resources.

Case study: wind farms At Coal Clough Wind Farm in Burnley, they use wind power to provide energy for their street lighting. They have received praise as part of the Energy Efficiency Scheme. As part of the local Agenda 21, Lancashire County Council is trying to use the idea of wind farms it has seen at Coal Clough within the county. This will help development without damaging the environment because carbon emissions will be cut by 25,000 tonnes per year.

Kyoto At Kyoto, Japan, in 1997, most industrial countries, including Britain and the United States, agreed to reduce their carbon emissions by between five per cent and seven per cent of the 1990 levels between 2008 and 2012. Developing countries said that they would do this later.

■ Change

In March 2001 President George W. Bush withdrew his country's support for the Kyoto agreement.

Mr Bush said that the agreement would harm the US economy and hurt American workers. It was unfair, he said, to expect industrialised countries to reduce carbon emissions when developing countries did not have to.

Later, Mr Bush said that there would be benefits for companies reducing emissions. The United States has five per cent of the world's population and produces almost a quarter of the world's carbon dioxide.

? questions

3. Write an email to President Bush saying what you think of his decision not to support the Kyoto agreement.

4. Find out what your local council is doing to help your local environment.

5. Explain what sustainable development is.

❖ keyword

Agenda 21
The name given to a plan of action signed by the government of almost every country in the world. Under this agreement governments and local authorities must develop special policies for achieving sustainable development.

Criminal law

The first topic in this unit explains how magistrates' courts work. These are local courts that hear a very large amount of all criminal cases heard in court.

Inside a magistrates' court

Press
Reports of a trial may be given in the local and national media. Sometimes the press are not allowed to reveal the names of children involved in a case. Victims of serious sexual assault are also protected in this way.

Witness stand

Legal adviser
A qualified lawyer who advises magistrates on the law. Known as the justices' clerk.

Probation service
Probation officers provide magistrates with reports on the social background of offenders. This helps magistrates decide on a sentence.

Public gallery

Magistrates

There are two kinds of magistrate: *lay justices* and *district judges*.

Lay justices are members of the local community. They work as magistrates part-time. They are unpaid, except for expenses. They have no legal qualifications, but do receive training. Lay justices are also known as *JPs*, or *justices of the peace*.

District judges do the same job as lay justices, but are trained and experienced lawyers.

Prosecution and defence

Lawyers for the prosecution and defence question each witness. They make opening and closing statements at the beginning and end of the trial.

If the defendant has pleaded or been found guilty, the defence will probably suggest why they should be given a lighter sentence – perhaps giving reasons why they acted as they did.

Defendant

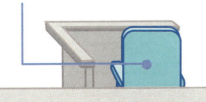

Court usher

The usher escorts witnesses to and from the witness stand and helps with the smooth running of the court.

On trial

■ Criminal proceedings

Arrest The police have the power to arrest anyone they reasonably suspect of committing a crime. That person can be held for up to 24 hours, but must then normally be:

- charged with an offence
- cautioned or
- released.

Advice Anyone who is arrested always has the right to see a solicitor. This is free and in private.

Charge If there is enough evidence, the police will charge the suspect with the offence.

The accused will then generally be released on bail and told when and where they are due to appear in court. If the offence is very serious, or the police believe that the suspect will not attend court, they can apply to a magistrate to have the suspect held in prison until the trial.

Summons This is an order issued by a court telling someone to appear in court on a certain date.

Crown Prosecution Service When the police have investigated an offence they pass the file to the Crown Prosecution Service. This organisation decides whether there is enough evidence for the case to go to court.

Magistrates' court All criminal cases are first brought to a magistrates' court. If the accused is aged 17 or under, the case will be heard in a youth court.

The more serious offences are passed on to the Crown Court if magistrates are satisfied that there is a reasonable case. In some cases, such as theft, defendants have the right to ask to be tried by a judge and jury. If the request is granted, these cases are passed to the Crown Court.

Crown Court A case in the Crown Court is heard by a judge, who makes sure the trial is run fairly. The verdict is reached by the jury and, if the defendant is found guilty, the judge passes sentence.

Help with costs The accused is entitled to help with the legal costs. This is funded by the Criminal Defence Service.

Criminal law

In court

The magistrate's tale

Michael Marks is a magistrate in Wolverhampton.

'I sit in court for about 40 days a year. Last Friday I had two cases of shoplifting, a man accused of shooting his neighbour's cat and benefit fraud.

'I've lived in this area almost all my life. I think the local knowledge that magistrates bring is invaluable.'

Most magistrates are:

- local
- unpaid
- have no legal training.

? question

1. What do you think would be a good and what do you think would be a difficult thing about being a magistrate?

Drink driving

This is one of the cases that Michael Marks had to deal with.

The defendant Rhys Hughes, aged 34.

The offence Driving a motor vehicle while over the alcohol limit.

Plea Guilty.

Prosecution evidence At 2 p.m., four days ago, the defendant drove his car into a parked car. No one was injured, but both cars were damaged.

The defendant was breathalysed. He had twice the legal level of alcohol in his system.

Defence statement Rhys Hughes had met his partner for lunch. She wanted to end their three-year relationship. After she left, Rhys continued to drink. The accident happened on his way back to work.

Mr Hughes has worked for his employer for 16 years. He thinks he will lose his job if he is sent to prison.

Sentencing

The defendant must be disqualified from driving for at least a year, and up to a maximum of three, unless there are special reasons not to do so. Magistrates may also impose:

- imprisonment for up to six months
- a fine of up to £5,000 (the average is £300–400)
- up to 100 hours' community service.

❓ question

2. Produce the magistrate's speech to Rhys in court having made your judgement. Include the following:
   - summary of the case
   - what your judgement is
   - what his punishment is and why.

Local justice

Strong efforts are made to ensure that magistrates reflect the local community.

There is the same number of male as female magistrates, but few from ethnic minorities and people under 40. In 2000, almost half the magistrates in England and Wales were retired and most had been in well-paid jobs.

❓ question

3. You have an appointment with your local councillor. You feel very strongly that the magistrate system is unfair because of the type of people (older, white and well off). Prepare what you would say to the councillor.

In court

Magistrates' duties

Magistrates handle more than 90 per cent of all criminal cases. They also deal with some civil cases (see pages 11–12).

Civil law cases include matters of family law, such as the care of children.

Other cases dealt with by a magistrate include:

- the non-payment of council tax
- granting licences for the sale of alcohol
- deciding whether a person who has been arrested should be allowed out on bail.

Youth courts

Specially trained magistrates also sit in youth courts, hearing cases involving young offenders (under 18s).

Powers

In criminal cases, magistrates can impose a range of sentences, including:

- fines of up to £5,000
- up to six months' imprisonment
- two years' detention in a Young Offenders Institution for under-21s.

Qualifications

Magistrates must:

- be between the ages of 27 and 65 when they are appointed
- live close to the area served by the court
- be of 'good character'.

❓ question

4. Design a job advertisement for a magistrate saying what personal qualities you think the person should have to make fair judgements. For example:

Magistrates wanted – must be:

1. _____
2. _____
3. _____
4. _____

Remember, magistrates do not get paid, but are thought well of in the community.

Criminal law

Crown Court
This second topic looks at the working of the Crown Court.

■ Trial by jury

Tessa received a letter calling her for jury service. Her name was chosen at random from the local list of voters. She has to report to the local Crown Court in six weeks' time. Jury service, it explained, will last a minimum of two weeks.

Tessa is not very keen to go. She is very busy at work. Having two weeks off will cause major problems.

She thinks it could be interesting to sit on a jury, but is worried about the thought of sending someone to prison.

Excuse me It is becoming more and more difficult to get people to serve on a jury.

Two out of three who are summoned for jury service either give reasons why they shouldn't serve, or simply don't turn up.

People from ethnic minorities and younger people are less likely to be called on for jury service. Many are not on the local list of voters.

? questions

1. What do you think Tessa should do? Should she take her place on a jury, or make an excuse and try to get out of it?

2. Do you agree with the statement, 'People who are called but won't serve on juries should be heavily fined'? Give reasons.

3. How would you feel if you were asked to sit on a jury? Would you be worried like Tessa?

Crown Court

■ Juries

A jury sits in a Crown Court. It decides on the guilt or innocence of the accused, based on the evidence it hears. A jury is made up of 12 adults, aged 18 to 70.

Ineligible Certain people may not serve on a jury. These are:

- people connected with the law, such as judges, magistrates, police officers, solicitors and prison officers
- anyone who is on bail or has been on probation in the last five years
- anyone who has been to prison within the last ten years
- ministers of religion.

Excused Some people are automatically excused. These are:

- MPs
- peers (lords)
- doctors
- members of the armed Forces
- people aged between 66 and 70.

Everyone else must attend unless they have good reason not to. Failure to attend may mean a fine of up to £1,000.

Finance People are not paid for jury service, but they can claim travelling expenses and money is available to help with loss of earnings.

■ Six weeks later

Tessa decided that it would be a shame to miss this chance.

She arrived at the Crown Court, joining the 30 to 40 other people who had been called on that day. They were shown a video, explaining what would happen in court.

15 people were chosen at random, including Tessa. They were led to Court 4, where a trial was about to begin.

Swearing in Inside the courtroom, another random selection was made. Twelve of the 15 people present were told to sit in the jury box. Again, Tessa was chosen. Each member of the jury was sworn in. Before this

happened, both the prosecution and defence could challenge the choice of a person, if they had good reason.

I'M NOT *#@•%#* SWEARIN' IN!

❓ question

4. Sometimes, blind or deaf people or those with learning difficulties are asked to serve on a jury. What are the arguments for and against letting them serve?

Criminal law

Cause of death

During her two-week jury service, Tessa heard three cases. The first involved assault and the second, dangerous driving. The third was a charge of burglary and manslaughter.

■ Accused

The defendant
Graham Eden, aged 26.

Charges
Burglary and manslaughter – that is, killing resulting from an unlawful and dangerous act.

Plea
Guilty to burglary. Not guilty to manslaughter.

■ The facts

On 16 January, Frank Bingham, aged 72, was alone in his house. At around 3.45 p.m. a brick smashed some glass in the front door. A man entered the house.

The man shouted that he was looking for cash. He went into the front room and started to search a cupboard. Mr Bingham said that he had no money apart from £15. The man took the money and left.

A witness later identified Graham Eden. She saw him running away from the house shortly before 4 p.m. His fingerprints were found on the front door and on several pieces of furniture. He was arrested two days later.

Immediately after the burglary, Mr Bingham telephoned the police. Three officers were at his house in less than ten minutes.

Shortly after the break-in, Mr Bingham was taken ill. He had suffered a heart attack and was dead on arrival at hospital.

Evidence

Prosecution The main witness called by the prosecution was Dr Geddes. He had examined Mr Bingham's body. He said that the shock brought on by a stressful event could last for at least an hour and a half.

Dr Geddes said he believed that the shock of the burglary brought on Mr Bingham's heart attack.

Defence Graham Eden did not give evidence. His lawyers called two witnesses – Dr Foster and Eileen Lewis, a neighbour.

Eileen Lewis said there was a lot of noise outside Mr Bingham's house after the burglary. She heard police sirens and loud banging as the door was being repaired.

Weighing up

The jury

The job of the jury is to listen to the evidence and to decide whether the defendant is guilty or not guilty.

Proof Members of the jury are told by the judge that they should reach a verdict of guilty only if they are really sure of the defendant's guilt.

Verdict A judge will ask the jury to reach a unanimous verdict (meaning they must all agree). However, if they take more than two hours to agree, the judge may call them back and tell them that a majority verdict of eleven or ten will be acceptable.

Secrecy Jurors are not allowed by law to discuss the case with anyone else.

Dr Foster, a heart specialist, said that stress caused by the burglary would have gone away after 20 minutes. It could not be a cause of death an hour and a half later. If anything, it was likely to be the noise afterwards that caused the attack.

Summing up

The judge told the jury that they must consider what they had heard very carefully. If they were certain that Mr Bingham died as a direct result of the burglary, they should find Graham Eden guilty of manslaughter. If they felt that Dr Foster may be correct, they should find him not guilty.

? question

1. Tell the story of Graham Eden's case and say what verdict you think you would have come to. Give reasons for your answer.

Civil law

This unit looks at the way in which a case of civil law may be dealt with.

Taking a case to court

■ On the bench

Mark plays five-a-side football every Monday night at the local leisure centre.

One evening a bench had been left by the wall on one side of the sports hall.

Mark noticed that the bench had been left out, but did nothing about it. Twenty minutes into the match, he ran straight into the bench. He fell badly on his right arm.

Mark spent the rest of the evening in casualty. He had a small cut above his eye, his shin was heavily bruised, and his right arm was broken.

Counting the cost Mark is a self-employed builder and, because of his injuries, had to take a month off work – without pay. He had two tickets for a music festival, costing £100 each. With a broken arm, he was unable to drive and the tickets were not used.

? question

1. Draw a storyboard of Mark's situation. Finish it by saying whose fault you think the accident was.

■ Next

Mark made an appointment with a solicitor.

Advice The solicitor said Mark had a good case for claiming **damages** against the local authority that ran the leisure centre. The staff there had a legal duty to make sure that the sports facilities were safe for people to use.

However, she said a case like this could take a long time and be stressful.

Costs His solicitor told him about the 'no win, no fee' scheme:

- Under this, Mark would not be charged a fee if his case did not succeed.
- If he lost the court case, he would probably have to pay the other side's costs, which could be at least £1,000.
- If he won he could receive several thousand pounds in damages. These could be reduced if the court decided that Mark had played a part in it.
- Under the 'no win, no fee' scheme, his solicitor's costs would be taken out of his damages.

Taking a case to court

■ Here to help

Citizens Advice Bureau (CAB) There are offices in most towns and cities. They give free and confidential advice on all kinds of problem.

Solicitors These are trained lawyers. They:

- give advice on legal problems
- take action on their client's behalf
- represent them in court.

The Law Society and the Community Legal Service (CLS) can help people find a solicitor.

Law centres Staffed by lawyers, they give advice. They may be able to take on a case like a solicitor, sometimes at a much lower charge. However, there are only just over 50 law centres in the whole of England and Wales.

Legal costs Arrangements to help people with the cost of civil legal cases have changed in recent years. Public funding is no longer available for help with certain types of legal problem, which include cases of personal injury. These are now handled on a 'no win, no fee' basis.

? question

2. What do you think Mark should do? Should he try to claim damages for his accident?

❖❖ keyword

Damages
Money awarded by a court to compensate someone for the loss or injury they have suffered.

Civil law

The County Court

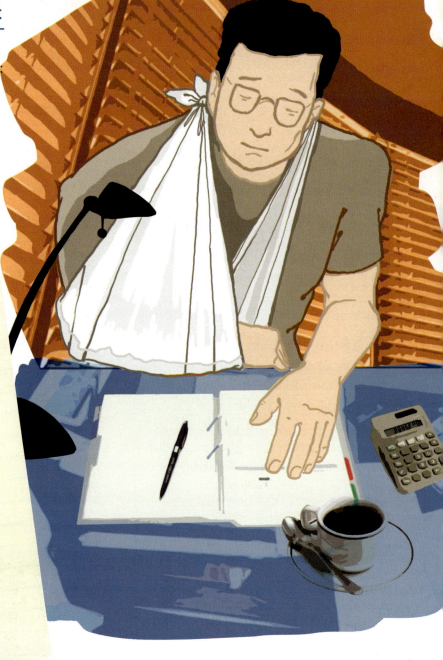

■ Seeking a settlement

Mark puts together evidence to support his claim. This includes:

- his account of what happened
- statements from two other players
- a doctor's report
- details of his losses.

These are sent to the solicitor acting for the local authority.

Special damages
Loss of earnings: 4 weeks at £450 a week £1,800.00
Replacing glasses, damaged in the accident £100.00
Taxi fares, when unable to drive £40.00
Music festival tickets, unused £200.00

General damages
Pain and suffering from broken arm, a badly bruised shin, minor bruising to the head.

Shortly afterwards, Mark's solicitor receives evidence from the local authority, showing why they feel they are not to blame.

■ Evidence in court

The case now moves to court – about six months after the accident took place.

Mark's solicitor is claiming that Mark's injuries were caused by the negligence of the leisure centre staff.

Proof Mark's solicitor must show that:

- leisure centre staff had a responsibility to make sure that the sports hall was safe
- they failed in this responsibility by not putting the bench away
- this caused Mark's injuries.

County Courts

County Courts deal with:

- civil cases
- broken contracts
- personal injury
- family matters
- divorce
- discrimination not connected with work.

Small-claims track This is a simple, informal hearing. It is designed to allow people to conduct their case without a solicitor. A judge listens to both sides and reaches a verdict.

This deals with:

- personal-injury claims up to £11,000
- most other claims up to £5,000, e.g. a holiday that did not live up to expectations.

Guidelines for damages All judges use the same guide when awarding damages for injury. The current guide states that damages for a broken arm should be between £3,500 and £9,500.

However, if the judge decides that Mark contributed to the accident in some way, the damages may be reduced. This is known as 'contributory negligence'.

question

1. Prepare the case for both sides that would have been heard in court. Copy and complete the table. Add your verdict at the end.

Mark's solicitor	Local authority lawyer
• Local authority should have made sure room was safe	• Mark saw the bench and didn't put it away

Verdict

In a civil matter such as this, the case must be proved 'on the balance of probabilities'. This is a lower level of proof than is required in a criminal court, where the jury must be sure that the defendant is guilty.

keywords

General damages
The name given to damages that cannot be precisely worked out – for example, the effect of pain and suffering.

Negligence
Careless action, or lack of action, causing someone loss or injury.

Special damages
Damages that can be worked out – for example, loss of earnings as a result of an accident.

GCSE Citizenship Studies

This unit is written specifically for those students who are taking the OCR GCSE Short Course in Citizenship Studies. It outlines the nature of the course and provides guidance on the examination and coursework.

The OCR course

The OCR GCSE Short Course provides you with an opportunity to obtain an approved qualification in Citizenship Studies.

The course consists of one tier covering grades A★ to G. Candidates who gain grades G to D will have achieved an award at Foundation Level. Candidates gaining grades C to A★ will have achieved an award at Intermediate Level.

Your Citizenship Studies course will probably be taught as a regular and separate timetabled subject. However, you are also encouraged to use information you have gained from other subjects as well. It is also worth remembering that any work you do either in school or the community may also be useful here – particularly as the basis for your coursework.

■ Coursework and the examination

Assessment for the course is divided into two parts – coursework and written examination.

Coursework   Candidates have to give in two pieces of coursework, which together make up 40 per cent of the total mark.

The written examination   This consists of one paper lasting 1 hour 30 minutes. It has three sections and accounts for 60 per cent of the marks.
• *Section A:* multiple-choice and short-answer questions carrying 20 per cent of the total mark.
• *Section B:* questions based on issues covered in the source book that will be sent to schools by the examining board six weeks before the examination. Candidates cannot take the source book into the exam, but a new copy will be given to them to use in the exam. This section again carries 20 per cent of the total mark.

Section C: questions based on a candidate's thoughts and understanding of action they have undertaken within the school and/or the wider community. This again counts for 20 per cent of the mark.

Assessment objectives   The three assessment objectives are set out in the course syllabus, as follows.

You will be required to:
• show your knowledge and understanding of current events; roles, rights and responsibilities; communities and identities; democracy and government; in a local, national and global setting
• find information from the media and say what it means; express your own opinion and be able to break down information and present your evidence on different issues, problems and events
• write about citizenship activities in which you have taken part, looking at what you and others did and how you have benefited from this and learned for the future.

Coursework

Candidates are required to submit two pieces of coursework for examination. Each one must not be more than 800 words in length and carries 20 per cent of the total mark.

The pieces are each referred to separately as *Coursework A* and *Coursework B*. They are quite different, and are explained in detail below.

■ Coursework A

Coursework A is an account of your involvement in a school- or community-based activity.

School-based activities include community or environmental projects, taking part in a play or other large project, being a member of the school council or a reading partner.

Community activities cover charity work, support for a local group, the Duke of Edinburgh Award or membership of a youth group or council.

In your account you must explain: what you did, why you did it, what you learnt from the activity, and what it did for others.

You must also outline the background and context of your activity and try to make sure that the examiner can see what you have learnt or gained. It is a good idea to highlight the problem that you faced and how you tried to overcome it. The examiner will also be interested to know how you might build on your experience.

You might also like to keep a diary or logbook of what you did and take some photographs to illustrate what the activity involved.

■ Coursework B

In *Coursework B* the exam board asks candidates to write an account comparing two sources of information on a citizenship issue of their choice.

Every section in this book is based on a citizenship issue of some kind, such as crime, race, poverty and the environment. A citizenship issue is a question that affects society as a whole, on which there is some disagreement over how to proceed. For example, *how should we care for the elderly?* or *who is responsible for reducing pollution?*

In your assignment you must:
• summarise the views expressed in each of the sources that you have chosen
• set the main issues in context, by explaining the background to the events in question and relating to the local, national, or global picture
• identify and explain any bias that is evident in your sources
• express and justify your views on the matter in question, and suggest how you think the situation might develop.

■ Supervision

You should receive guidance from your teacher – particularly when selecting the topic for your coursework and drawing up an overall plan. However, your reflections, judgements and conclusions must be all your own.

■ Presentation

At the end of your coursework you should give a bibliography (list of any books/sources used) with the name of the author, title of the book and the name of the publisher. Anything directly quoted should be shown using speech marks.

All work submitted for moderation must be in an A4 flat card file or document wallet, not a ring binder. Mark your work with the:
• centre number
• centre name
• candidate number
• subject title and code
• assignment title, i.e. *Coursework A* or *B*.

Volunteering

There are great opportunities for getting involved in, or volunteering for, community activities. If you are not clear about what you would like to do, help is available from a number of websites, including Community Service Volunteers *(www.csv.org.uk)* and the National Centre for Volunteering *(www.volunteering.org.uk)*. These give ideas and guidance on volunteering opportunities in your own area. There is also a Volunteer Bureau in most towns and cities. Details are available from the phone book and your local library.

There are certain practical questions that you will also need to consider. How much time can you afford? Are you able to make a regular commitment, or would it be better to volunteer for just one event? How far are you prepared or able to travel? Will you make the arrangements alone, or would you prefer to volunteer with a friend?

You will also need to plan how you will use your volunteering experience in your coursework. This is likely to involve background research and a discussion with the organisers or the people with whom you volunteer. You may also need to go back to assess the impact or effect of what you have done.

Remember, there are many opportunities in your school or your area to get involved. Are you a form captain? Have you raised money at school? Are you on the school council? Have you organised a school activity or taken part in an assembly?

GCSE Citizenship Studies

The examination

The paper is divided into three sections and candidates are expected to answer all questions. All three assessment objectives (see Pages 140–1) are tested in the paper. *Sections A* and *B* test assessment objectives I and II. *Section C* tests objective III.

■ Section A

The questions in this section are made up of:
- five multiple-choice questions, each worth one mark
- ten short- or one-word-answer questions, each worth one mark
- four short-response answers, two worth two marks, and two worth one mark.

Put a ring around the **Multiple choice** Put a ring around the number of the definition (1 2 3 4) that matches the term.

A1 What is meant by the term *globalisation*? (1)

1. A global agreement to encourage sustainable development.
2. A move towards a single currency for members of the European Community.
3. A declaration of the United Nations to encourage greater international security.
4. The trend for large businesses and the media to operate across the world.

Short or one-word answers

A2 State what is meant by the term pressure group. (1)

A3 State one way in which a political party differs from a pressure group. (1)

Short-response answers

Sam buys a plastic model kit for her son, Danny. She gives it to him when he gets home, and he starts to put it together straightaway.

Danny soon realises that a piece is missing. Sam checks to make sure it has not fallen on the floor and decides that the kit must have been incomplete when she bought it.

Sam asks your advice on what to do next.

A4 Circle the statement (1, 2, 3) that gives the best advice and give one reason to explain why you have chosen it.

1. Send the kit to the manufacturer and ask for it to be exchanged for one that is complete.

2. Report the matter to the police.

3. Take the kit back to the shop and ask for her money back.

Reason

....
....
....
....
....   (2)
....

■ Section B

Section B has four questions – two each worth six marks, and two each worth four marks.

Some weeks before the exam you will receive a source book. Your teacher will help you understand the information in this booklet and you will be allowed to make notes. You cannot take the source book into the exam, but you will have gone through it before with your teacher.

Questions in section B require you to show that you are able to understand and interpret the information in the source book.

B1 Study Document 4 and answer the question that follows.

Document 4

Halim's story

Halim is a journalist from Algeria. Two years ago he wrote a series of articles criticising those religious groups who were trying to stop Algeria from becoming too Westernised. He said the people should be allowed to adopt Western values if they chose to, and that religious hardliners were wrong to try to prevent women from having more rights.

From then on, it seemed, Halim was a marked man. There were two attempts on his life, his newspaper's office was bombed and threats were made to his wife and child.

He asked for protection from the government. Help was promised, but his life became no safer. Government officials themselves were often targets for attack.

Under the pretence of going on a family holiday to Egypt, Halim took his wife and daughter to Cairo and then on to London, where he claimed political asylum.

Using Source 1 from your source book, explain whether Halim would be likely to qualify for refugee status in the United Kingdom. Give one reason for your decision. (4)

Source 1

The Convention Relating to the Status of Refugees, passed by the United Nations in 1951, defines a refugee as follows:

A refugee is a person who is outside their country and cannot return because of a well-founded fear of persecution for reasons of race, nationality, membership of a particular social group or political opinion.

Someone who does not fully meet this test may still be allowed to stay by being given Exceptional Leave to Remain. This is a special agreement that allows a person to stay in Britain if sending them home would seem to be very cruel or unkind.

■ Section C

Section C has three questions worth two, three and fifteen marks.

The fifteen-mark question requires an essay-style answer and carries an extra four marks for communication skills, making it worth nineteen marks in total.

C1 Using examples taken from your studies and from any school or community action that you have taken part in, state three things that you could do in a democracy to influence decision makers. (3)

C2 'All young people, at some stage in their school lives, should be required to undertake voluntary work of some kind.'

Write an essay to show how far you agree with this statement. (15)

In your answer you may use examples from your studies and from any school or community action project that you have taken part in.

Index